# THE
# FORT

## GROWING UP
## IN GROSSE POINTE
## DURING THE CIVIL RIGHTS
## MOVEMENT

# Douglas J. Vrieland

Trimble Hollow Press

Unless otherwise indicated, all Bible passages are from the New International Version (Grand Rapids, Zondervan, 2011). Unattributed photos by the author.

Published by Trimble Hollow Press, Acworth, Georgia


ISBN: 978-1-946495-28-0
eISBN: 978-1-946495-27-3

Cover Art by Cathryn M. Green
Cover Design by Trimble Hollow Concepts

*This Book is Dedicated to*

*Curtis Jay Vrieland, my father*

*and*

*The memory of Reverend Franklin D. Steen, ThD,*
*my pastor in Junior High and High School.*

*I was blessed to have a godly father*
*and a faithful pastor*
*during the turbulent years of the late 1960s.*

# Table of Contents

# Acknowledgements

Three years ago, while I was walking down Eighth Street in Holland Michigan, I saw a woman working on her painting in the window of the Holland Arts Council building. The painting was of the Farmer's Market in Holland and was loaded with detail. Fascinated, I stopped in to chat with this painter. That was the beginning of a relationship that grew as we engaged in a number of chats about art. I discovered she was the author of several books, including *Ninety Brothers and Sisters* in which she tells of growing up in rural Kentucky in a Christian orphanage owned and operated by her abusive father. That was the spark that led to the idea of telling my own story about growing up in the all-White suburb of Grosse Pointe during the Civil Rights Movement. Lenore DePree "helped me find my voice," and challenged me to see writing as an art-form. Her encouragement in those early days when I asked her to read a few pages of the first chapter were invaluable.

Two other experiences led to the writing of this book. I had the privilege for a short time of serving on the anti-racism committee of Creston Christian Reformed Church in Grand Rapids, MI. From that experience I realized that I had a story that the next generation to fight racism needed to learn. The members of the committee also taught me a great deal, especially by their encouragement to attend the two-day intensive workshop offered by the Congregations Organizing for Racial Reconciliation (CORR). I found that workshop difficult but invaluable. I realized how little I knew about African American history in America, and determined to learn more. I thank both Creston Church and CORR for what they taught me.

As I was contemplating writing this book, I found myself in the office of Jul Medenblik, President of Calvin Theological Seminary where I am an alumnus and my daughter was a student. He listened as I expressed my frustration in ministry and my upbringing on the streets of Detroit and Grosse Pointe, a background much different from those who grew up in communities with a large Dutch population. He offered his encouragement, and I walked out of his office with several books about the history of Detroit during the Civil Rights Movement under my arm, books which at the time of this writing I still need to return. Thank you, Jul, for your support and encouragement.

The Council of the First Christian Reformed Church of Detroit gave its enthusiastic support to the project. My thanks to the church's pastor, Ben Van Arragon, and the Council President, Mary Kalmink, for their support throughout the project, for reading what I thought was the final manuscript and for offering their valuable insight. Special thanks to Helen McDonald, the last Principal of the Grosse Pointe Christian Day School and now the Director of God's Kids, a Christian pre-school operated by the church. Her patience with me as I interrupted her work so that she could take me to the School archives was both noticed and appreciated.

I had interviews with a number of people who were a part of this story, and whose memories have been preserved for future generations. Included in this list are David Cooke, Sr. and Dave Cooke, Jr., Tom Van Wingerden, Miriam Schaafsma, Jack Nyenhuis, Stacey Steen, Shirley Verspoor, Kathy VanderBrug, Duane VanderBrug, Mel VanderBrug, Suki Botts, Bill VanderVliet, Jarrett Bel, and my father, Curtis Vrieland. I appreciate the e-mails from Richard Grevengoed, which were especially helpful with their description of his year at the Community Church in Detroit.

I must mention Reverend Doctor Cornelius Williams, interim pastor of the Second Baptist Church of Detroit, and his love and support. I enjoyed our times together sharing decades of experiences in ministry. You have become a friend, and I wish you well as you finally move into retirement.

Special thanks to Wendy Pollitt for reviewing my manuscript and making numerous grammatical corrections. You are a great English teacher, and I am a better writer because of your help. I apologize for the numerous sentence fragments. I really do believe they are a part of my "style."

My "McDonald's" coffee friend Bill Schoonveld deserves mention for his help with the Dutch language and history. I tried to follow his wise advice, for which I am grateful: "Never let history get in the way of a good story." While I tried hard to maintain historical accuracy, he impressed on me the importance of telling the story in an engaging way.

My brother-in-law and his wife, Doug and Terri McKittrick, who helped me with the publication and taught me the mechanics of publishing. Thank you for helping me avoid the many pitfalls that first-time writers are liable to fall into.

I want to give a very special thanks to my precious family: my wife Robin, my children Becky, Heather, and Sean, and their spouses. Thanks for putting up with my never-ending stories and listening to my exciting (to me) discoveries about Detroit. I love you all and appreciate your patience and support.

Finally, I give thanks to my God to whose glory I try to live my entire life.

# Preface

In an America increasingly divided over race and religion, the Christian church finds itself at a crossroads. Traditionally, Protestant Christianity (and particularly Christianity in the Reformed tradition) has been a religion of words. Christians consider themselves the sum of the beliefs they can put into words. Christian salvation is a matter of publicly articulating the correct formulations of words. Christian mission is scattering words of faith upon an unbelieving world in the hopes that at least some of these words will find a receptive heart in which to germinate.

Increasingly, faith in the ability of our words to influence others and impact our world is naive. Not only is our culture saturated in relentless verbal messaging – through 24-hour news outlets, viral videos and torrential tweetstorms. But the pervasive spread of fake news and deliberately divisive rhetoric has hardened even the most accommodating heart. No one takes anyone's word for anything anymore.

All is not lost. Christians can still influence the world for the better. But to do so we must learn, with creativity and integrity, to translate our believing into doing. When the Christian church is at its best, it does three things:

It presents a compelling vision of a better reality.

It introduces a God who is passionate about making life better for the most vulnerable.

It impacts the world for the better.

In *The Fort,* Douglas Vrieland introduces a church that, albeit imperfectly, did all three. During an era of racial and religious division,

Doug's childhood church aligned itself with a movement that refused to accept the world as it was and fought for what could be. It did so on the basis of its long-standing commitment to the Bible and its conviction that the God of the Bible is uniquely committed to the cause of the vulnerable and the marginalized. It participated in a movement that made the broader world better. In the process it broadened the narrow world of its congregation, communities and constituents for the better. Doug recounts the way his childhood church stepped out of the close confines of its building, traditions and neighborhood to engage the cause of justice in the world outside its walls. So doing, it inspired a boy to follow a parallel course. It was in the church – that oft-misguided and increasingly oft-maligned institution – that Doug was a given a vision for a better world, a better way to live in it, and a God who makes life better.

For more than a decade I have served as pastor at Doug's childhood church. I have seen the church grow in numbers and diversity. I have overseen the faith formation of its newest, youngest and oldest members. I have celebrated moments in which the church chose hospitality and generosity over prejudice and self-preservation. I have grieved moments in which it chose silence, comfort and tradition over protest, risk and innovation. I dream of this church, and others like it, taking the kinds of courageous stands Doug witnessed here during his childhood. Because of the story Doug tells, I believe it still can.


Ben Van Arragon

July 2020

First Christian Reformed Church of Detroit ("The Fort") and Grosse Pointe Christian Day School (bottom, left). Photo courtesy of First Christian Reformed Church of Detroit.

*I feel very sorry for anyone who does not live in Detroit."*

-Grace Lee Boggs[1]

*Was it worth trying to show the one race what went on behind the mask of the other?*

-John Howard Griffin[2]

# Introduction

In the movie, *The Last Samurai,* Tom Cruise plays a US Army Captain, veteran of the Indian Wars, who accepts an assignment to go to Japan and teach the Emperor's army how to use modern weapons. In his first battle with the Samurai, Cruise is captured and taken to a remote spot where he meets Katsumoto, the Samurai leader, and learns "the way of the sword," the Samurai traditions of warfare. The film focuses on the conflict between the traditional Japanese ways represented by the enemy Samurai warriors with their swords, and the modern Western ways represented by Cruise with his pistol. The brilliance of the movie lies in the fact that there is no right and wrong in the story. The modern Western ways have some advantages over the traditional Japanese ways, but they come with a price. Japanese traditions, filled with symbolism and meaning, have been replaced by Western ways that have no connection with the past. The Samurai robes, rich with color and meaning, have now been replaced with a modified version of the western uniform. The connection with the Japanese military past and the history that formed the proud culture of the islands has been severed. In the future Japan will not be protected by the traditional Japanese warriors, but by a western-style military. In the final scene of the movie the Emperor says, "I have dreamed of a unified Japan, of a country strong and independent and modern. And now we have railroads and canons. Western clothing. But, we cannot forget who we are or where we come from."

This book is *The Last Samurai* story, only set in Detroit. It is the story of a small, relatively unknown religious community during the last four years of the 1960s. It was a traditional community whose ways, like the Samurai's at the beginning of the Meiji era in Japan a hundred years earlier, were being challenged by the social turmoil that was going on in the city around them. The religious community was called the First Christian Reformed Church of Detroit, an all-White congregation located near the intersection where the wealthy Grosse Pointes connect to the big, industrial city of Detroit. It is the story of a godly father and a faithful pastor who were both part of the community and whose visions often collided. It is a story of a spiritually sensitive young boy with deep admiration for both.

The lives of the members of this congregation centered around their church and a Christian School located behind the church building. The church's massive edifice anchored by a corner tower without a steeple and its function as a place of safety and refuge for its members lie behind the metaphor for the congregation that serves as the title of this book: *The Fort*. Like all Americans, the members of this community were challenged by the massive societal changes of the 1960s. The biggest of these for this Detroit-area community was in the area of race relations. The civil-rights movement as it developed in both Detroit and Grosse Pointe forced the community to reevaluate its beliefs, values, and beloved ways of doing things. Some, like the Samurai, placed great value in the culture and traditions that had served them well in the past. Others advocated for new ways to meet the challenges of a rapidly changing society.

This story is a very small piece of the much larger American story that is both common and unique. Ethnic-religious communities struggling to maintain their traditions in the face of new challenges existed throughout the country. The same story with different details could be set in an Irish Catholic community in New York City, a Scotch Presbyterian community in Pittsburg, a German Lutheran community in Milwaukee, or the Polish Catholic community of Hamtramck, Michigan. My story of growing up in an ethnic-religious community in Grosse Pointe is also a unique story. It is not the only story that could be told of growing up in that exclusive lakeside community during the Civil Rights movement. The experience of a young boy growing up in one of the other churches and attending either a Catholic or Public School would be a much different story, as would the story of someone growing up in one of the exclusive mansions close to Lake St. Clair. I tell this story because it is my story.

Just as 1960s, America is currently in the midst of rapid social change. In 1955 Will Herberg could write, "The outstanding feature of the religious situation in America today is the pervasiveness of religious self-identification along the tripartite scheme of Protestant, Catholic, Jew."[3] That is no longer true. The American religious scene includes Islam among the monotheistic faiths, as well as a host of non-monotheistic religions, people who believe in God but don't subscribe to any organized religion, others who claim to be spiritual but not religious, and a growing number of Atheists. Today's America is home to a higher percentage of people with darker skin and an LBGTQ community far more visible and vocal than it was at the time of the Stonewall uprising in 1969.

In this environment, arguments seem to be useless. Arguments for and against abortion rights, second Amendment rights, how to maintain border security, how to divide and spend the healthcare dollar, whether or not climate change exists, and a host of other issues have been made over and over again with little progress. We are not a nation united, as the Emperor dreamed for Japan. We are a nation divided, entrenched in our positions. The issues are generally portrayed in Black and White terms, with such broad values as faith, justice, and equality used on both sides to support their position. Those who disagree are clearly wrong; our side is clearly right. We have a national language as binary as computer code.

In such an environment we need to remember who we are as a people and from where we come. The best way to do this is through the telling of stories. For those open to serious reflection, *The Last Samurai* tells a powerful story. It is my hope that the telling of the story of The Fort will similarly benefit those who carefully reflect on the lessons available from this piece of Detroit history.

This is a story about race. It is a story about a Caucasian community responding and reacting to the African American struggle for racial equality. I recognize that this is one of the most sensitive issues of our society, and that the potential for misunderstanding and further wounding of people who have suffered is high. African Americans have especially suffered and continue to suffer from the evil of racism. While I can never fully understand what it is like to live in America with Black skin, I have made a concerted effort to learn as much as possible. I have spoken with numerous African American leaders and have done extensive reading on the African American experience and history, especially in Detroit.

One of the questions I had to face in writing this story is how to refer to African Americans. As is demonstrated in the newspaper articles and other sources quoted, in 1967 the common word was "Negroes." Later the word "Blacks" became more common, and today the usual term is African American. After consulting with African American leaders, especially pastors, I have chosen to use the term "Negro" when describing the historical events of the late 1960s; otherwise I have used the term "African American," or occasionally "Black."

African Americans are not the only ones who have suffered from the scourge of racism. The White community of Grosse Pointe has also suffered and continues to suffer. The legacy of racial intolerance has left hidden wounds, including but not limited to the spiritual wound of shame, a difficult burden for such a proud community to bear. The risk of re-opening wounds with yet another book on the past racism of Grosse Pointe is great. But wounds sometimes need re-opening in order to get rid of infection. The full story needs to be told, a story of courageous people that took great risks to do the right thing, of people that had honest disagreements as to what the right thing was, and of people frightened that they might lose the gains they had worked so hard to achieve. As Dr. King said on that historic evening of March 14, 1968, when he spoke at Grosse Pointe High School:

> I want to discuss the race problem tonight and I want to discuss it very honestly. I still believe that freedom is the bonus you receive for telling the truth. Ye shall know the truth and the truth shall set you free. And I do not see how we will ever solve the turbulent problem of race confronting our nation until there is an honest confrontation with it and a willing search for the truth and a willingness to admit the truth when we discover it.[4]

In this book I discuss the race problem very honestly if not as eloquently as Dr. King.

I acknowledge that my perspective is that of a Dutch American male who was raised in the upper middle-class White community of Grosse Pointe Woods. I have benefitted my whole life from what has been referred to as White privilege. I know that speaking about White privilege will immediately turn off some readers, but in my case, it is clearly a fact. I come from a family that valued education and I have had the privilege of attending private schools. I have never known real poverty, and as an adult have received unearned respect and credibility simply because of my skin color, national origin, and gender. I never asked for this privilege, but I have it. The only thing I have any control over is how I use it. In this book I try to use my privilege, like John Howard Griffin did nearly sixty years ago in his book *Black Like Me,* "to show the one race what went on behind the mask of the other." My hope is that this book will facilitate greater understanding between those whose skin is Black and those whose skin is White.

There is more that unites us as Black and White Americans than separates us. Dr. King said it well in his speech in Grosse Pointe: "Whether we like it or not culturally and otherwise, every White person is a little bit negro and every negro is a little bit White." The African American underground railroad conductor George DeBaptiste is as much a part of my story as the Dutch immigrant leader Albertus Van Raalte, because they are both a part of the American story.

There are not "good guys" and "bad guys" in this story. Just complex characters full of fear and hope, anger and vision. Some were frustrated by the inability of the community to move forward. Others were afraid of where the church was going. Many times, people on both sides were tempted to leave, to affiliate with people who were more like-minded. Some did, but most were committed to each other, and so they stayed and worked to find common ground. At times they came up short; other times they took bold and courageous steps forward. Their common value system, which for them was a Biblical Christianity out of the Reformed, Calvinist tradition, was what guided them. I was formed in the crucible of this authentic, nitty-gritty, street level orthodox Christianity.

I write this story for a new generation that will take up where my generation leaves off. The Detroit rebellion of 1967 was relived in Ferguson, Missouri in 2014, where a predominately Black community once again rebelled against a predominately White police force. At the time of the Ferguson unrest I was living in Japan, serving as a chaplain with the United States Navy. My heart broke as I read the story. The nation I love and have served has still not learned the important lessons of Detroit, 1967. And so, as a military chaplain who for the last 20 years has worked with the amazing young men and women of this country who will soon take baton of leadership that my generation must hand off, I offer my story. It is a Christian story because I am a Christian, but it is not written solely for Christians. I have tried hard not to preach. What I have tried to do, especially in the epilogue, is to offer a few conclusions.

My story is a true story, at least as far as it is possible to tell such a story more than fifty years after the events. Memories get clouded with time. Biases get confused with the actual events. But there are no fictional or composite characters in this story. Some details have been omitted and names have been withheld to protect people's privacy. This is primarily a story of faith and of how faith guided a religious community during turbulent times. It is a story written to encourage the reader's reflection, and to help us all once again learn the important lessons of the Civil Rights movement as it was played out in Detroit and Grosse Pointe, Michigan.

*"Nineveh has more than a hundred and twenty thousand people who cannot tell their right hand from their left, and many cattle as well. Should I not be concerned about that great city?"*

-Jonah 4:11

*The Dutch would bring a most valuable class among us, if they selected our state as their destination.*

-Judge Romeyn

# Chapter 1

# Alter and Mack

Little did I know on that snowless February Sunday in 1966 when I first entered The Fort what adventures lay ahead. I knew about a War in Vietnam: mealtime prayers always included the petition, "Be with the men and boys in Vietnam." But as a White boy growing up in the Dutch-American communities of West Michigan, I knew nothing about Civil Rights; nothing about Montgomery, Birmingham, or Selma. I had never even heard about that far-away place called Alabama, about Rosa Parks or Dr. Martin Luther King, Jr. I knew nothing about a March on Washington. My innocent childhood mind was filled with dreams, but they were dreams that were far different from those of Dr. King. I was a boy dreaming of adventure. Especially the new adventure our family began three days earlier. The adventure of living in what my mother called "a nice neighborhood." Of living in a house with a (half) bathroom on the main floor and a real family room. The adventure of exploring the metropolitan area whose map I had studied; communities with names like Lincoln Park, Allen Park, Highland Park (so many "Parks"), five Grosse Pointes and a Grosse Isle, Hamtramck, Harper Woods and St. Clair Shores. Adventures of riding city busses and of exploring new streets on my one speed Murray bicycle. Adventures of shopping at J.L Hudson's in downtown Detroit, the second largest department store in the world and sponsor of one of the Thanksgiving Day parades we watched at grandma's house. Dreams of our family bundling up and attending that parade some year and of being on TV. These were the dreams of a nine-year-old boy, centered around what life will be like in the big, exotic city of Detroit, far away, on the opposite side of Michigan's mitten from our old home in Kalamazoo.

Nor did the people who squeezed into the pews and overflow seats of The Fort that Sabbath morning know the pilgrimage we, they and I, would take together over the next eight years; a pilgrimage in which their lives and mine would intersect and be influenced by historic events that would make national news: race riots, Dr. King's "Other America," the national debate about forced bussing for racial desegregation. On that Sunday, they knew nothing of these future adventures, nor did they know then that I, child of that new family in town, would one day become a "Son of the Church," a great honor given to any congregation that has one of its boys grow up to become a minister. They did not know how deeply the tensions of the next eight years would affect this child's dreams of living a rewarding life as a missionary in some faraway place like Africa, a dream that was just as spiritual to me as the dream Dr. King articulated at the end of the Walk to Freedom March in Detroit in 1963 and later on the steps of the Lincoln Memorial. And they did not know on that day that this boy's dream would culminate in that mysterious, almost mystical vision the people gathered at The Fort that day believed in but couldn't quite explain. They simply referred to it as "the call," a divine injunction to enter full-time ministry as the pastor of a church.

The worshippers that gathered in The Fort knew nothing of these things as they gathered. What they did know was what they believed. They believed whole-heartedly in the Christian faith. Their faith was formed and nurtured by the teachings of the sixteenth century Protestant Reformer, John Calvin (1509-1564). From Calvin they learned that God was Sovereign over all of life. God was the King, the Ruler of the Universe. Jesus Christ was Lord. According to Calvin, the human

2

problem was that they have rebelled against God's authority, which was sin against God. These worshippers believed in the need to acknowledge and to repent, which for them meant to turn away from their sin. They believed the death of Jesus Christ on the cross nearly 2,000 years earlier allowed God to grant them forgiveness. They believed that those who embraced Christ would have their sin washed away by His blood and be granted salvation or a new life. This new life was not just something they would experience someday in heaven, but also something they were to live out on a daily basis in this world. Their challenge was to now live this new life of obedience, motivated by love and gratitude for what God had done for them in Jesus Christ. Calvin's teachings were embraced by the Dutch during the Reformation and were the theological basis of the Dutch Reformed tradition. The worshippers in The Fort that Sunday morning knew who they were: Dutch, Calvinistic Christians.

They also knew that they were gathered in The Fort that Sunday morning not to dream but to gain spiritual strength and refreshment through worship. They were there to worship that Almighty, Sovereign God they believed in, using the familiar patterns and rituals that were so meaningful to their Dutch Reformed souls: singing from the blue *Psalter Hymnal* (the only hymnal approved by the denomination for use in Sunday worship) accompanied by the massive pipe organ; hearing the Ten Commandments read out of the King James Version of the Bible; confessing their sinfulness, being assured once again that forgiveness could only be found in the work of Christ on the cross; having the pastor bring their personal burdens and the burdens of the world before what they called the Throne of Grace (from which God ruled); and most importantly receiving instruction from God's Holy Word, the Bible. The service ended, as always, with the pastor raising his arms and pronouncing God's blessing on these Detroiters:

*The Lord bless thee, and keep thee:*
*The Lord make his face shine upon thee, and be gracious unto thee:*
*The Lord lift up his countenance upon thee, and give thee peace.*
*Amen.*

To which the congregation responded by singing the doxology, a traditional and well-known song of praise:

*Praise God from Whom all blessings flow,*
*Praise Him all people here below,*
*Praise Him above Ye heavenly hosts,*
*Praise Father, Son, and Holy Ghost. Amen.*

No one had the slightest inkling of how God would in fact not only bless them but also make them a blessing to that nine-year-old boy, and to people throughout the city, across the country, and around the world in the years to come.

Two historical events set the stage for the future drama that would be played out in and around The Fort. They are two very different stories of ethnic communities who picked up and moved in search of freedom. Two Stories drawn from the Great American Story, of which they were a part: one a small paragraph in the chapter entitled "Immigration," tucked between the founding of the 13 Colonies and the establishment of Ellis Island; the second, a major section of the chapter entitled "The African-American Experience."

The first is the story of The Great Trek,[5] a nineteenth century re-enactment of the American Thanksgiving Day legend of 1620-1621. William Brewster is played by Albertus Van Raalte, a Calvinistic minister. The English Pilgrims become the *Afgescheidenen* (a Dutch word usually translated as "Separatists"). *The Mayflower* is now *The Southerner*. Plymouth, Massachusetts becomes Holland, Michigan.

4

The part of the friendly Wampanoag Indians is played by the Odawa tribe, "good" Indians who help the White settlers and ensure their success. The plot centers on a spiritual community intent on re-creating Calvin's Geneva, a community in the Promised Land of America living under God's laws. Like any good remake, 'The Great Trek" includes an interesting twist in the story. In the original version, the English Puritans spend time at the beginning of their pilgrimage in the Netherlands, where they were warmly welcomed but feared cultural and spiritual danger to their children if they continued to live among the Dutch Reformed Calvinists whose crude, guttural language their children were beginning to pick up. In the 1846 remake, the Dutch Puritans spend a winter in Detroit, where they are warmly welcomed by the leaders and members of the First Presbyterian Church, the spiritual heirs of the English Pilgrims. Like the English before them, the Dutch leaders of The Great Trek were worried about the cultural and spiritual dangers they would face if they settled in the big city of Detroit (population of over 9,000 people). These farmers had already journeyed through New York City, Albany, and Buffalo, all of which had large Dutch settlements. They never for a moment considered ending their pilgrimage in Detroit, a mixed community of French and English settlers that served as the capital of the State of Michigan. Instead, after wintering in Detroit they moved across the state of Michigan and created their own settlement, which they named Holland. In 1857 these American Separatists broke away from the Reformed Church in America with which they originally affiliated and formed the Christian Reformed Church. The Fort was one of the congregations that formed the Christian Reformed Church (CRC).

The Dutch farmers of the Great Trek intended to settle in Wisconsin, but when the political, religious and economic leaders of the young state of Michigan learned of their presence in Detroit they made a concerted effort to encourage them to settle in their state. As Judge Romeyn of Detroit wrote: "the [Dutch] would bring a most valuable class among us, if they selected our state as their destination."[6] The state leaders hosted Van Raalte on a trip across the state in December, 1846, and met at First Presbyterian Church in Detroit on January 22, 1847, where they committed themselves to the support of the Dutch colonists. The state leaders were successful in their efforts, and with money loaned to him by these leaders Van Raalte purchased 3,000 acres for $7,000 in order to establish his colony.[7]

A mile and a half southeast of First Presbyterian Church on Fort Street was the congregation of the Second Baptist Church of Detroit, who met in a rented hall. They were also hosting new arrivals to Michigan in that winter of 1846-1847. The Second Baptist Church had been established ten years earlier, in 1836, when 13 former slaves who were no longer willing to be relegated to the "nigger pews" of the First Baptist Church, who were upset about not being allowed to be baptized in the same waters as the White members, and who felt betrayed by their fellow White church members during Detroit's first race riot, the "Blackburn Rebellion," walked out and established a new congregation. Their current location, just a few blocks from the Detroit River separating the United States from British controlled Canada, became the final stop on the Underground Railroad for runaway slaves. There is no record of political figures suggesting that these newcomers would "would bring a most valuable class among us, if they selected our state as their destination." Rather the laws of the day, including the Constitution of the United States,[8] and the Fugitive Slave Act of 1793[9] required that these runaway slaves be apprehended and returned to their owners.

The same year Van Raaalte arrived at First Presbyterian, a man named George DeBaptiste arrived at Second Baptist Church. DeBaptiste

was born to free Black parents in Virginia and had served as both a personal valet to General William Henry Harrison and as a steward in the White House during Harrison's brief presidency. After serving President Harrison, DeBaptiste lived in Madison, Indiana where he ferried runaway slaves across the Ohio River from the

Statue of George DeBaptiste pointing the way to Canada to a group of runaway slaves. Hart Plaza, Detroit, Michigan.

slave state of Kentucky to the free state of Indiana. In 1850, soon after Van Raalte led his Dutch settlers west on a train to Holland, DeBaptiste, who was something of an entrepreneur, purchased a steamship, the *T. Whitney,* and hired a White man to pilot it. The *T. Whitney* was used both for commercial purposes and to secretly transport former slaves to Canada and freedom.

The second historical event that set the stage for the next eight years of The Fort's journey is the story of the Great Migration, an American drama that was still playing in 1966. It is a story starring a primarily African American cast seeking not religious freedom but freedom from the oppressive restrictions placed on them in the Jim Crow South. The drama opens with an announcement by Henry Ford on January 5, 1914, that he would pay his workers $5 a day. Other big, northern cities dotting the shores of the Great Lakes, cities with names like Buffalo, Erie, Cleveland, Milwaukee, and Chicago also offered high wages in their industrial factories that at the time were producing materials for the First World War. But Detroit was the most prosperous city of them all, and it became the Promised Land for these African-American farmers that had already experienced so much suffering. And so they migrated north, by the hundreds during and after the war. [10] Their dream, like that of the Dutch before them, was for a place where they could peacefully settle down and raise their families without harassment. The support cast in this drama includes hundreds of White southern farmers who also made the journey north in search of a better life. They brought with them the Jim Crow mentality of the segregated south.

Van Raalte's land grant from the State of Michigan would not be sufficient to support all the grandchildren and great-grandchildren of those who made the Great Trek, and they began to migrate eastward to the big city of Grand Rapids to find work in the factories and in the building trade. When the news of the high wages being offered in Detroit reached these Dutch workers, who were making $12.00 a week, some of them decided to move to the Motor City. Others who made their living in the building trades saw an opportunity building homes for all the newcomers to Detroit. And so the Dutch and the offspring of former slaves once again cross paths in Detroit. In 1914 these new Dutch settlers petitioned the denomination to form a church, and the First Christian Reformed Church of Detroit, "The Fort," was born.

The Great Trek and the Great Migration: two dramas starring unnamed Emmy winning actors described on the Statue of Liberty as simply "your tired, your poor, your huddled masses yearning to breathe free."

The Fort stands on the residential corner where Goethe Street dead-ends into Maryland, in the northwest corner of Grosse Pointe Park. It is a church named for Detroit but located in Grosse Pointe. The members came from both Detroit and Grosse Pointe. Two blocks east of The Fort is Alter Road; one block north is Mack Avenue.[11] Alter and Mack, two streets that form the boundary between Grosse Pointe and Detroit. The Grosse Pointe Park neighborhood surrounding The Fort is known as the "cabbage patch," its modest single family and duplex houses with no room for driveways between them stand like soldiers in close order formation. This humble neighborhood looks more like one of the neighborhoods of Detroit than the more exclusive neighborhoods of the Grosse Pointes. The Fort stands tall and proud in the cabbage patch, near the intersection where Alter and Mack cross, serving the spiritual needs of two very different communities.

To the south and east is Grosse Pointe. Or rather, the Grosse Pointes. Five independent cities: Grosse Pointe Park, City of Grosse Pointe, Grosse Pointe Farms, Grosse Pointe Woods, and Grosse Pointe Shores. Once known as the Newport of the Midwest, the "Pointes" are five exclusive communities that sit comfortably along the shores of Lake St. Clair. Here you will find the "old money" of Detroit: the mansions of automobile pioneers like Ford, Packard, Olds and Dodge stand proudly on Lakeshore Drive looking over Lake St. Clair, with senior executives and successful white collar workers populating perfectly manicured neighborhoods that diminish in prestige the further you get from the lake. Five communities with five separate police forces and five private lakefront parks open only to residents. Five communities that, to use the language of the day, were "lily White."

To the north and west is Detroit. The Motor City. Automobile Capital of the World. Arsenal of Democracy. American Dream city in 1950 with the highest per capita income of any major city in the United States. Factories. Rows of single-family homes and two or four family "flats" inhabited by blue-collar workers. The Promised Land calling Southerners to migrate to the cold north. A city with its own Central Park, beautiful Belle Isle, located on an island in the Detroit River between the United States and Canada. Home of the United Auto Workers (UAW). A city with a strong Mafia presence. A city struggling with racial tension. The city that in the next decade would become the Murder Capital of the nation. Motown. Crack houses. America's Third World city.

The Fort stands in the shadow of the corner where these two very different worlds come together, Alter Road and Mack Avenue, guarding those within her walls from the twin threats of the idolatrous materialism of Grosse Pointe and the urban problems of Detroit.

Compared to the church I had come from, a simple colonial style building with square windows and maple woodwork, The Fort was a massive Cathedral. A Calvinistic Cathedral. An imposing Neo-Gothic brick structure, [12] The Fort occupied two city lots like a 300-pound man squeezed into an airplane's single economy seat. Years earlier Goethe Street next to The Fort had been closed and turned into a parking lot. Unfortunately, this parking lot was large enough for only about a third of the worshippers that assembled on Sunday morning. Those who arrived early parked their cars side by side in the normal fashion. The cars of later arrivals were parked in two lines in the access lane between the two rows of parked cars. My parents had never experienced such a parking arrangement and debated whether they should follow the others lead and block in their fellow worshippers. It didn't take long for my parents to decide that they would conform to this strange practice.

The truth is that my family, not knowing that we had to leave early to secure a seat and perhaps not knowing how long the commute was from our new home to our new church, were late that Sunday morning. "Late" was defined at The Fort (as in many churches of that day) not in relation to when the service began but when the seats were filled. This transgression resulted in two punishments: we had to park in the aisle of the parking lot and therefore could not linger very long after the service and talk, and we were forced to sit on metal chairs set up to the left of the pulpit in full view of the rest of the congregation. We were never late again.

The interior of The Fort projected an aura of grandeur, mystery, and even spookiness. The first thing that struck me on that first Sunday was the darkness of the church. It wasn't a problem of lighting. The traditional gold and white chandeliers found in so many houses of Christian worship easily provided enough light for the worshippers to read the words in their hymnals and Bibles. The darkness was in the woodwork. The pews were stained a dark black walnut, a melancholy color that enveloped the worshipper, a color that symbolized the darkness of sin and evil that Calvinists took so seriously. There was no center aisle. The pulpit and chancel area were approached not directly but from one of the two off center walkways that split the pews into three sections. The three-point doctrinal sermons were delivered to the three sections of worshippers from a pulpit as dark as the pews. The wall above the pulpit and the three chairs behind the pulpit were stained with the same dark walnut color, the latter upholstered in a dark maroon imitation leather fabric. Behind the chairs was a matching walnut rail that marked off the walnut paneled chancel, a dark, unused space. No choir loft. Only an open Bible centered on the back wall, with a small reading light shining on its opened pages, almost hidden by the pulpit from which the teachings of this Sacred text were proclaimed faithfully twice every Lord's Day.

The darkness, however, only came so high in The Fort. Above the darkness of the pews the three-story walls were painted a clean white, creating a brightness reminiscent of a Vermeer landscape painting. On three sides of the sanctuary stood massive painted-glass windows filled with Christian symbols, allowing light to penetrate the interior of The Fort. Above the dark woodwork on top of the pulpit were the organ pipes, standing proudly with the tallest in the center and descending on either side to the shortest. On the front wall on either side of the organ pipes were false window frames encasing two Bible Verses from Psalm 96. On the congregation's left were the words: *Sing unto the Lord, bless His name.* In the frame on the right side were the words: *"Show His salvation from day to day."* The sanctuary expressed visually the hope of the congregation: *"The light shines in the darkness, and the darkness has not overcome it"* (John 1:5). Christ is the Light of the World, a resurrection Light that defeated the midday Good Friday darkness of the cross. The only possible response was praise and song.

My nine-year-old faith did not yet grasp the profound theology being subtly taught by the architecture of this Reformed Cathedral, devoid as it was of any pictures or statues that might hint of Catholicism. All I saw was the darkness. And the overwhelming grandeur of the three-story-high auditorium. This was the sanctuary of The Fort, the safe place offering spiritual shelter for those who needed a break from the trials and struggles of life. Eventually I came to experience the safety of that place and to understand the power of the message taught there as the believers struggled with the darkness of a broken, hurting world. But on that first Sunday morning all I felt was an anxious curiosity about what this Sacred Place in the heart of the massive metropolitan Detroit area was all about.

Singing was a very important part of worship in The Fort, but there were strict rules that had to be followed. I never heard of the Pentecostal practice of "dancing in the aisles." Such a practice would be unimaginable to a congregation of stoic Dutch men and women. Congregational singing gave opportunity to express deeply felt emotions, and the people sang with unashamed feeling and enthusiasm. Four songs were chosen for Sunday morning worship from the *Psalter Hymnal*.

The *Psalter Hymnal* was a unique hymnbook: the first 310 songs were based on the Psalms found in the Bible. Historically Calvin's followers would only sing lyrics that came from the Bible, as they were seen to be from God Himself. But eventually the American practice of singing hymns made its way into the Reformed churches, and so both Psalms and Hymns were combined in the hymnal—both a *Psalter* and a *Hymnal* in one book. In The Fort on Sunday mornings, two songs were always from the Psalm section and two were hymns.

As a boy, I quickly learned how to tell the difference. The numbers for the chosen songs were posted on a board behind the organ. Any number less than 310 was a Psalm, anything over 311 was a hymn. For the most part, I much preferred the hymns. Few of the Psalms had catchy choruses that I liked to sing. There were exceptions. Number 13, from Psalm 8, with its upbeat tune in 6/8 time and catchy chorus was a favorite of us kids:

> Lord, our Lord, in all the earth, how great Thy Name!
> Thine the Name of matchless worth, excellent in all the earth,
> How great Thy Name"

And number 304, from Psalm 148, with its funky countermelody in the chorus:

> Let them praises give Jehovah, for His Name alone is high,
> And His glory is exalted, and His glory is exalted.
> And His glory is exalted far above the earth and sky.

Many of the Psalms, however, were much slower and subdued, offering opportunity to express the more painful emotions of shame, hurt, sadness and anger. Psalm 51 was often chosen following the reading of the commandments. We would join the adulterer David in confessing our sinfulness:

> God, be merciful to me, on Thy grace I rest my plea.
> Plenteous in compassion Thou, blot out my transgressions now;
> Wash me, make me pure within, cleanse O cleanse me from my sin.

> I am evil, born in sin; Thou desirest truth within.
> Thou alone my Savior art, teach Thy wisdom to my heart;
> Make me pure, Thy grace bestow, wash me whiter than the snow.

The worst Psalms in my mind were those written by someone called Louis Bourgeois. The adults called them the "old Dutch Psalms." To me they seemed to go on forever. They were usually written with lots of whole or half notes, and often took up two pages in the hymnal. They were typically based on what the adults called the "imprecatory psalms." I later learned the term "Psalms of lament" for these emotion-filled

songs. The heaviness of the words—one could hardly call them lyrics—
added to the torture.

> *Out of the depths of sadness, O Lord, I cried to Thee;*
> *Thou who canst fill with gladness, lend now Thine ear to me.*
> *O Font of consolation, attend unto my cry,*
> *Hear Thou my supplication and to my help draw nigh.*

Meanwhile, less than ten miles away on West Grand Boulevard in a
converted house with the sign *Hitsville* out front, Berry Gordy Jr. was
producing cutting edge music under the Motown label. The Temptations
were offering a much different prescription for facing the struggles of
life:

> *I've got sunshine on a cloudy day*
> *When it's cold outside I've got the month of May*
> *Well I guess you'd say*
> *What can make me feel this way?*
> *My girl (my girl, my girl)*
> *Talkin' 'bout my girl (my girl)* [13]

Compared with songs like this being played on radio station CKLW
out of Windsor, Canada, the Dutch Psalms were melancholy and boring.
I didn't mind the sermons, but I dreaded it when, looking up the songs
during the prelude, I learned that we would have to sing one of the Dutch
Psalms.

The hymns were much more appealing. They were generally faster
and more uplifting. The Psalms had veiled references to Christ, but in
the hymns we could sing directly to Jesus. Some of them even had
choruses (called "Refrain" in the *Psalter Hymnal*), which I liked. They
were always sung in four-part harmony accompanied by the organ.
Sometimes there was an interlude before the final verse when the key
would change; on other occasions one of the verses was sung a cappella.

And on very special occasions the piano would join with the organ.

One of the major adjustments anyone moving into a cross-cultural setting has to make is the adjustment to new attitudes about time. We discovered early on that the Detroit church handled time in a much different way than the West Michigan congregations with which we were familiar. For example, the evening service began at 6 p.m., an unbelievably early hour according to our West Michigan sensibilities, where all the churches started at 7. This Liberal practice (Liberal being defined as "different" in our home) took a bit of adjustment for our family to get used to, especially since we would regularly spend the weekend either in Grand Rapids or at my Grandparent's cottage on Gun Lake. We either had to make the three-hour drive before 6, which meant rushing through the non-liturgical rituals of the Sabbath—coffee and sermon discussion after the morning service followed by Sunday dinner, missing out on a nap altogether—or wait until after 8 to begin the journey, which put our arrival at home at a late hour. I remember discussions about whether it was even appropriate to make such a journey on the Sabbath, but these were generally resolved by an appeal to the importance of family relationships. So naps were sacrificed on weekends when we visited Grandma and Grandpa.

The other strange thing about the marking of time at The Fort was the location of the clock. There was nothing notable about the clock itself, a typical institutional white-faced round clock with black numbers, hands, and frame. But for some unexplained reason the clock was located, not behind the congregation where the pastor could keep his eye on it, but on the side wall in full view of the entire congregation. This worked against the pastor in a number of ways. If the sermon was particularly dull, having the clock in such easy view made the time go even slower. And if the sermon was short (which only happened in the evening service), it led the congregation to the unmistakable conclusion that the pastor hadn't worked very hard the previous week. Either way, I fully understand the motives of whatever pastor had it moved sometime after I left for college.

The sermon was the center focus of the entire service. And it was supposed to be long, at least according to the way a child marks time. I remember one Sunday being especially aware of how long the sermons were. My widowed Grandma, a Lutheran from the Scandinavian community of Ludington on Lake Michigan, came to church with us. She was the only person I ever remember who followed the "Order of Service" that was professionally printed on the back of the bulletin cover, as unchangeable as the law of the Medes and Persians. I knew from our bi-annual visits to Ludington and Grandma's Lutheran Church—a wonderful edifice built in the 1950s with a beautiful picture of Jesus pulling Peter out of the water framed by the split pulpit—that for Lutherans worship services were printed out and required the worshipper to navigate a small library's worth of books. This was not necessary in our Reformed church. Everything was pretty much the same week after week, and those things that changed—namely the song numbers—were announced twice by the pastor: "Our hymn is number 451, *Take Time to be Holy,* verses 1 and 4. Number 451." No need to ever consult the Order of Service. But my Lutheran Grandma apparently needed the security of the Order in front of her in order to worship properly. On that particular Sunday I sat next to Grandma and her Order of Service and followed along with her as the congregation observed the familiar rituals. They moved along at a nice clip until THE SERMON. At that point, time came to a complete stop.

During THE SERMON the pastor would carefully explain the historical background of a chosen Biblical text or one of the finer points of Reformed doctrine. Textual sermons and doctrinal sermons were the two major spiritual food groups that sustained the congregation week after week, and each Sunday included a generous serving from both. The morning sermon was generally the textual sermon, based on a single text taken out of the Scripture reading of the day. The pastor would solemnly read the Biblical passage, and then pronounce: "Our text is verse 17," which was again read. No one ever questioned the pastor's authority to single-handedly choose "our text" for all of us. Once announced and re-read, this text was then divided into three points, with illustrations from the broader Scripture passage, the book in which the passage was found, the entire Bible, and finally (if he got to it) real life. This final point was called "The Application," and gave the faithful guidance for Christian living during the coming week. There was no need for an Altar Call, which everyone knew was an Arminian practice. The unstated assumption—which was from time to time vehemently denied—was that everyone in attendance was a Christian and the purpose of THE SERMON was to give guidance on how to be a good Christian. Of course, no one said it that way. They used the proper theological term: Sanctification.

THE SERMON in the evening service was generally a doctrinal sermon, based on one of the 52 Lord's Days of the Heidelberg Catechism.[14] This sacred document was found in the back of the *Psalter Hymnal* between the Belgic Confession of Faith[15] and the Canons of Dort.[16] Unlike the Confession and Canons, the Heidelberg Catechism was used on a weekly basis. Like the morning, the evening service included a Scripture reading. About half the time this was taken from the Book of Romans. Following the Scripture reading, the pastor would say: "In connection with this and similar passages from Scripture, turn to the Heidelberg Catechism, Lord's Day 45." This created a major problem. In my scholarly studies at the Christian grade school I had learned Roman Numerals, which headed each of the 52 Lord's Days. However, it was still difficult for me to decipher this foreign language, especially when it had an X next to an L or an I next to a V. By the time I had done the necessary advanced calculus, the pastor was halfway through the reading of the Catechism lesson. After this reading we once again were treated to THE SERMON, again in three points, usually more obvious than the points of the morning as they correlated quite well with the questions of Catechism. If we were lucky the clock on the sidewall had not yet hit seven when he said "Amen."

I never learned what my Lutheran Grandma's feelings were about our Calvinistic services, with those long sermons. She was a woman of deep faith, but she preferred not to talk about either her personal faith or the church. But the experience did make a lasting impression on me as to how long those sermons really were.

The pastor of First Church, Reverend John Groenewold, did not have a job description. Everyone knew what he was supposed to do. Monday was his day off. Tuesday through Friday mornings were to be spent in his study, preparing the two messages for the coming Sunday, and no one was to interrupt him unless it was a dire emergency. Afternoons were reserved for visiting the sick, shut-ins, and widows. Tuesday afternoon he would come to the Christian School located behind The Fort and teach Catechism classes to the children. This was another new experience for me, as our church in Kalamazoo did not start Catechism until a later grade. Lessons came from hard-covered books that included a couple of pages of reading, some questions to be answered on paper as homework, and a couple of questions and answers that had to be memorized. Rote memorization was the preferred method of instruction—at least by the adults. The class began with each student reciting the answer to one of the questions asked by Reverend Groenewold. No one wanted to be the first student called on any question, as the recitation of the answers by the first students would help stimulate the memory of those questioned later. I don't remember any of the questions or answers I supposedly memorized in those catechism classes. After reciting the memory work, we would go over the written answers to the questions from the previous lesson, and then if there was any time left, we would take turns reading the material from the new lesson. Things changed during my later years in the Christian School when Catechism was rescheduled for after school. The Junior High class had catechism at 3:30, a full half hour after school was out. This allowed us time to walk the block to Mack Avenue where, on the corner of Mack and Maryland stood Verdunct's Bakery. Every Tuesday my mother gave me eight cents, which allowed the purchase of a doughnut.

Preach on Sunday, catechize the Youth, and visit the sick. That was the pastor's job. The focus was inward and upward, caring for the flock that gathered inside the walls of The Fort every Sunday and making sure they understood the need for repentance and confession of sin, the wonders of God's grace demonstrated on the Cross of Jesus, and the importance of godly living, defined as personal and individual piety. Community involvement, speaking out on social issues like war and peace, poverty or racism-- these were not the concern of the church. "Liberal" churches, influenced by Marxism, focused on these things. In our church, the focus was on the Gospel and insuring individuals would spend eternity in heaven.

The Fort served two very important purposes for its members in those days. Detroit was a rough, even violent town. Violence among the automobile workers was common, both within the plants and on the picket lines during strikes. The mafia maintained a strong presence in both Detroit and Grosse Pointe, bringing a more hidden form of violence. The Ku Klux Klan was strong, bringing both violence and an anti-Catholic agenda.[17]  When The Fort was built in 1924, the Klan's write-in candidate for mayor, John W. Smith, almost won the primary election.[18]  Meanwhile, Henry Ford was spewing ugly anti-Semitic propaganda in his private paper, the *Dearborn Independent*, articles that were translated into German in a book entitled *The International Jew: The World's Problem*, a book Adolph Hitler kept handy on his shelf for ready reference.[19]

Racial tension was an ever-present reality in Detroit. The first race riot in the city, the Blackburn Rebellion in 1833, occurred four years before Michigan became a state. The "Sweet Trials," following the shooting of a White man in a mob surrounding the home of Ossian Sweet in 1925 drew national attention.[20] In 1943, racial tension erupted in what became the largest race riot in American history up to that time, a riot that started on Belle Isle, required 6,000 federal troops to dispel, and left 34 dead.[21]  In 1967 Detroit became the only city in the nation to be occupied twice by federal troops following the rebellion in July.

The Fort, and the Christian School behind it, served as a safe haven for its members and their children from such violence. Or at least gave the illusion of being a safe haven. It also served an important visual reminder to the congregation and perhaps for the surrounding community. In 1966 under the leadership of Mayor Jerome Cavanaugh, Detroit was seen as the "Model City" and "the City that Works." The race riots that hit Harlem and Philadelphia in 1964 passed by Detroit and hit Watts in Los Angeles in 1965. According to *Fortune* magazine, "Of all the accomplishments in the recent history of the city, the most significant is the progress Detroit has made in race relations."[22]    But racial tensions simmered beneath the surface and the nation was entangled in an unpopular war in Vietnam.    In times of prosperity and times of tension, the belfry of The Fort stood high and tall over the houses of the neighborhood and could be seen for several blocks.    This belfry, the highest point in the neighborhood, was a reminder of the God of these Calvinists, a God who was Sovereign over all.

On that snowless Sunday in February the members of First Christian Reformed Church faithfully gathered for worship, God was in control, and all was safe in the neighborhoods around Altar and Mack.    That security would be tested in unimaginable ways over the next eight years, beginning with that long week in July 1967.

*What happens to a dream deferred?*

*Does it dry up*
*like a raisin in the sun?*
*Or fester like a sore—*
*And then run?*
*Does it stink like rotten meat?*
*Or crust and sugar over—*
*like a syrupy sweet?*

*Maybe it just sags*
*like a heavy load.*

*Or does it explode?*

-Langston Hughes

*"It is not desirable to cultivate a respect for the law, so much as a respect for the right."*

-Henry David Thoreau

*"We can never achieve a free society until we suppress the fires of hatred and turn aside from violence, whether that violence comes from the nightriders of the Ku Klux Klan or the snipers and looters in Detroit."*

-Lyndon Baines Johnson[23]

# Chapter 2

# Two Miles From The Battlefront

Grosse Pointe reaches the height of its grandeur in mid spring. Magnolias, dogwoods, and flowering crabapple trees burst out with bold color in late April, offering aesthetic relief from the grey Michigan skies of February and March. The ride down Charlevoix Avenue every morning on the way to school in April and May was a journey through an art museum featuring nature's finest work. This initial splash of color was followed by the classy magnificence of June, with the first flush of the season's roses. Front lawns were perfectly manicured carpets of green, the color kept bright and pure from the damaging yellow of dandelions by Scotts Turf Builder. Red geraniums were the flower usually featured in the front yard in those days, a flower that offered the proper dignity and class required by such an exclusive community. I loved the spring, although my allergies did not.

Summer was a special time in Grosse Pointe with five lakefront parks featuring swimming pools and marinas, one for the residents of each of the five Pointe's exclusive use. We lived in Grosse Pointe Woods, the newest and least exclusive of the five Grosse Pointes. "The Woods" was the only one of the Grosse Pointes that did not include Lake St. Clair shoreline, and so at some time the city had purchased a large tract of lakefront property in Grosse Pointe Shores and developed a lakefront park, or as our family called it, the "pool park." The Woods boasted of having the largest pool among the five private parks. It was more of a small lake, divided into three sections by two buoyed ropes. The first section, stretching from the changing house to the first rope, was the shallow part. It was used primarily by infants and toddlers, their mothers watching closely, seated on beach chairs in the water hoping to get a tan. The middle part was the most crowded. The water was about two or three feet at the first rope and gradually deepened to five feet along the second rope. The third section, beyond the second rope, was the diving section. Two concrete docks, each maybe 20 feet long, jutted out into the water, creating the first opportunities for kids to jump into the deep water and later opportunities to learn to dive. At the far end of the pool from the pool house were the two most popular attractions, two diving boards creatively named the "low dive" and the "high dive." On a summer day there were lines of shivering kids (the water was not heated) waiting for their turn. Graduation to the "high dive" was a rite of passage for any kid, almost as significant as the completion of high school.

The Grosse Pointe Kiwanis Club ran busses painted in the Kiwanis Blue color from the neighborhoods of Grosse Pointe Woods to the pool park, offering free transportation for the community's children. On a warm day the 9:00 and 10:30 a.m busses had a respectable number of children aboard, but the 1:00 p.m. bus, right after lunch, was the most popular. The buses left the park in the afternoon for the return trip at 3:30 and 4:30, the latter bus being filled beyond capacity. On really hot days they scheduled an extra bus at 5:00. To my knowledge no kid was ever left abandoned at the park.

Sometimes my Mom would pack a picnic and she and Dad would meet my siblings and me at the park around 5:30 for supper and a swim. The typical menu featured tuna salad with canned pineapple chunks and what mother called "shoestring potatoes," those potato sticks that come in a can. The salad was held together with Kraft Miracle Whip—not the low-fat kind you can buy today, but the real thing that was so familiar to

26

our mid-western palates. The salad was served with cinnamon rolls from Awrey's, a major Detroit area mass producer of baked goods. Awrey's cinnamon rolls could be found in any local grocery store and came on a square disposable tin wrapped in cellophane. A big jug of Kool-Aid completed the menu. To us, this was a banquet worthy of serving in the finest palace. Supper would be followed by a swim, the pool being nearly empty since the hordes of kids had gone home on the "3:30 and the 4:40" (for some reason we never used the word "bus" when referring to the bus schedule).

In addition to the swimming pool, entertainment was provided by swings, slides, monkey bars, and fake animals atop heavy spiral coils that rocked back and forth. Sometimes we would take a walk along the boats moored in the marina. I loved looking at the sailboats, cabin cruisers and yachts. We would laugh together at the funny names the owners had chosen. My Dad's favorite was named "Pop's Wad." I never quite understood why that was funny. I didn't realize until later that a "wad" was a bundle of cash. By seven o'clock we kids would head home with Mom, while Dad returned to the office for a couple of hours more work. My dad worked hard to support his family and had little patience for those who didn't.

Many of those who did not have a boat on Lake St. Clair had summer cabins and cottages up north. Traffic on I-75 northbound on Friday and southbound on Sunday occasionally came to a halt when the Zilwaukee drawbridge north of Saginaw would open. My grandparents had a cottage on Gun Lake, between Grand Rapids and Kalamazoo. Our family typically traveled west rather than north on summer weekends and so were able to avoid the I-75 traffic and the Zilwaukee bridge. When I was around 10 years old, I was old enough to take out the 12-foot rowboat with its red 7 ½ Johnson Sea Horse engine by myself. At that point the entire lake was mine to explore. Mornings and evenings were reserved for fishing with Dad, trolling for small and largemouth bass. On other weekends we would go to my grandmother's house in Ludington, four blocks from Sterns Park on the shore of Lake Michigan. Afternoons lying on the Lake Michigan beach, walking on the breakwater or "uptown," and watching the Car/Train Ferries come in and out of port in Ludington provided all the adventure I needed.

For William Scott III (also known as "Billy") summers were much more challenging. I never knew Billy personally, but have come to know him through his memoir, *Hurt Baby, Hurt*.[24] Billy, a twenty-year-old African American, lived in the Virginia Park neighborhood of Detroit, twelve miles and a world away from our Grosse Pointe Woods home. While our home had at least some air conditioning—a window unit in each of the three bedrooms and one in the family room—homes in Virginia Park had no such luxury. Neither did Billy have access to a private pool park. My siblings and I took swimming lessons every summer. Billy, like most African Americans, never had such an opportunity and most likely didn't know how to swim. If he did want to cool off in the water, there was no free bus sponsored by the Detroit Kiwanis Club. He would have had to take at least two city buses, requiring a transfer, to Belle Isle where he could bathe in the polluted Detroit River. Kids in Billy's neighborhood did not have boats or summer cottages that they could escape to. While I cut the grass for our well-off neighbors in Grosse Pointe and eventually developed a nice little business, in Virginia Park the housing stock consisted of four story apartment buildings rather than single-family homes. Brick and cement were more common than grass. Between 25% and 30% of Black youth Billy's age were unemployed.[25] Summers were long, hot, and boring.

28

Billy was about ten years older than I was. He was as sensitive as I was. Unlike the privileged ten years of my life, Billy's two decades had been filled with struggle. His father was abusive and neglectful, and his mother, even before her death when Billy was 14, was frequently in the hospital. Billy was an easy target for bullies. His teachers called him "dumb," an epithet he came to accept. "Dumb Billy" was a follower, not a leader. The person he followed was his older brother Reggie.

I had two parents who made sure I attended church every Sunday where the Ten Commandments were read. Every Sunday morning, I heard, *Thou shalt not steal.* (Exodus 20:15, KJV). Billy's moral training came from Reggie. One of Reggie's favorite games was shoplifting. Nothing serious, but little things like taking a banana from an open-air market when the owner wasn't looking or stealing small items from the downtown department stores. About half the time they got caught, but Billy continued to follow his brother. Billy believed that, of the two of them, Reggie was the one with brains, and so he followed. Right into juvenile court, where they were given a caseworker from Catholic Social Services. The caseworker recommended taking Billy out of the home because of "family problems."

At ten years old I was exploring Gun Lake in a rowboat with a 7½ Sea Horse motor, 150 miles away from our Grosse Pointe Woods home. Billy was living in the Hawthorn Center, the first psychiatric centers for children in the nation. He was one of only two Black children at the center, which was located in Northville, 40 miles from his home in Detroit.

My father worked hard to support the family. He was blessed with a mid-level executive job that he enjoyed and was more than willing to return after supper to the office for a couple more hours of uninterrupted work. Billy's father was not as fortunate. His grandfather, William

29

Scott I, was one of the Great Migration immigrants of World War I and had a good job working at the Dodge Main factory in Hamtramck. But Billy's father, the second William Scott, was never able to get one of those good jobs in the automobile industry. Opportunities for work for Negroes were not as abundant by the time he came along. At that time, the last automobile factory to be built in the city of Detroit opened in 1929. The Big Three (GM, Ford and Chrysler) built twenty new factories during the decade between 1946 and 1956, but these new factories were all located in the suburbs, especially along the Mound Road Industrial corridor.[26] Black people were denied suburban housing because of their skin color, and public transportation from the inner city to the suburban factories was poor, limiting inner-city Black people's opportunities for work. When William Scott II couldn't find work in the plants, he turned to other means of employment available to him at the time, including hustling "the numbers" and running an unlicensed drinking establishment.

At the time it was very difficult for African Americans to get a license to serve alcohol. So unlicensed Black entrepreneurs developed "Clubs" to serve the market for music and alcohol at night and on the weekends in areas like Twelfth Street. In the Clubs male patrons could also find women who for a price would provide a particularly enjoyable form of stress release. Scott's Club, at 9125 Twelfth Street at Clairmont, was one such unlicensed establishment. It was located in the space leased by the United Community League for Civic Action (UCLCA). The UCLCA was operated by William II and his brother, a college graduate whose political efforts helped get Mayor Cavanagh elected with 85% of the Black vote. After the election, there was little activity at the UCLCA, so Scott opened a club during the off hours.

My grandfather had a high school education and was a self-employed as a small businessman. My father earned a bachelor's degree and worked as a mid-level executive for a life insurance agency. I would eventually earn a Doctor of Divinity degree and work full-time as a Christian minister and military chaplain. The three generations of William Scotts charted a different path. William Scott I, autoworker at Dodge Main. William Scott II, hustler providing booze, gambling and women. William Scott III, patient in a child psychiatric center.

The downward spiral of poverty.


Hawthorn Center was good for Billy. He felt safe there. The atmosphere was wholesome—no junkies, winos or prostitutes. The buildings were clean and new. The staff was loving and caring. Differences between people were settled without fighting. Billy, who never liked violence to begin with, thrived in the atmosphere at Hawthorn and developed an aversion to violence.

After three years at Hawthorn, Billy was made a ward of the court. He was moved to the Boys Republic in Farmington, another institution for emotionally disturbed children, because the cost of the private Hawthorn Center was too high for the state to pay. At Hawthorn Billy had been one of only two Black children. At Boys Republic he was one of many. At fourteen, like any other teenager, he was trying to figure out his identity, but his emotional struggles made this difficult. And now he had to navigate a new challenge: being Black. He was no longer unique like he had been at Hawthorn. Now he was just another Black boy, whatever that meant. Billy hated Boys Republic, began to hate himself for being Black, and developed a strong desire to be a White child.

But Billy learned values at both Hawthorn and Boys Republic that offered the promise of being a decent person and being accepted by others. These values included respecting one's elders, obeying the law without question, and not cheating, lying or stealing. Keep away from bad company and immoral people, and don't have sex outside of marriage. Work hard and you will be successful—that's the American promise. And make sure you go to church every Sunday.

Billy did attend church every Sunday at Boys Republic, and he did his best to follow the religious and moral ideals taught there. He believed what the church taught him, and he believed that because of his religiosity he was a better person than the other Black boys at Boys Republic.

After three years at Boys Republic, Billy had progressed as far as he could. So, plans were made for his discharge. But to where? His mother was dead, his older sister pregnant. Reggie was still institutionalized, and his father was busy running the numbers and his club. So sensitive, religious Billy was placed in the foster home of Mr. and Mrs. Kane, a Black couple on the east side of Detroit. Two other foster boys, Joey and Gary, were already living with the Kanes.

Mrs. Kane was strict and abusive. At first her abuse was aimed at Joey and Gary. Billy was the well-behaved religious boy who didn't need punishment . . . until Mrs. Kane found a stain in his underwear. Billy had discovered girls, and his attraction to one of them and an unintended release of tension caused the stain. Mrs. Kain was certain it was Billy's active behavior that produced the stain and pronounced her verdict: "You nasty-ass Black nigger." She hit him in the head with a broom handle, told him that from now on he had to wash his hands six times before coming to the dinner table because "ain't no tellin' what you been doin'," and grounded him for two weeks. As she turned away, hormone filled Billy had tears in his eyes.[27]

After the meal Billy went and found a phone booth, called his father, told him what had happened and that he wanted to come home. His father told him to come straight home, so he caught a bus back to 12th Street, a place he had been away from for six years. Mrs. Kane lost her foster care license.

Billy's return to Twelfth Street was not easy. The values of the street were different than the values he had acquired out in the suburbs. The fighting and stealing that were an everyday part of life went against Billy's hatred for violence. He kept himself neat and clean and spoke properly. He believed in God and country. People began to call him names: "Proper" and "Whitey." While he didn't like the names, he did believe he stood out from the others as a decent person who was clean and maintained "proper thoughts." And he continued to attend church— an Episcopal church across the tracks from his house, filled with middle-class Black folks. This not only alienated him from the others on 12th Street, but also from his own father. Billy believed in obeying the law. His father made his living hustling numbers and running an unlicensed club. Although nothing was said, the older Scott knew his son disapproved of his lifestyle.

However, William Scott II did encourage Billy to continue his education. Billy loved school and wanted to learn. While at the Kanes, he had successfully finished the summer session at Eastern High School, taking the bus across town every day. In the fall of 1963 Billy began at his new school, Northern High School, an all-Black school on Woodward and Clairmont. Still eager to learn, he discovered that many of the teachers cared little about the academic success of their students and did little actual teaching. At the beginning of his final semester Billy was assigned vocational courses rather than college prep courses and had

33

to threaten to quit school before the counselor changed his schedule. "Don't say I didn't tell you when you don't graduate on time," were his final words to Billy on the matter. Billy did graduate on time and went on to study for a year at Michigan Lutheran College on Woodward Avenue.

One year after Billy's graduation another student at Northern High School, Ivory Williams, sat in a guidance counselor's office and like Billy before him asked that he continue on the same college prep track in his senior year that he had pursued throughout his high school career. The guidance counselor told him that they were not sending Northern students to college, that the city needed more service workers. Williams walked out of the counselor's office with a schedule that included woodshop, metals and automotive classes. The implication was that Northern students would not go to college because they were Black. Several days later, at a lunch table discussion, Williams learned that others had received the same message: they would not be allowed in the necessary classes that would prepare them for college. He and three of his classmates made an appointment with the school's principle, Arthur Carty, to discuss the matter. Carty called them "Niggers" and threw them out of his office.[28]

That same spring another student at Northern named Charles Colding wrote an editorial for the school newspaper entitled "Education Camouflage." He pointed out a number of inequities at Northern High compared to other schools in the Detroit system: overcrowded classrooms, inadequate facilities and counselors, and a faculty of mostly White teachers who discriminated against Black students. He wrote about the practice of social promotion and aggressive behavior by the on-campus police. Colding concluded that the differences in achievement between the students at Northern compared with such predominately White schools as Redford High needed to be addressed. According to Colding, the belief among White teachers and administers was that "Negroes aren't as capable of learning as Whites."

The head of the English Department, Thomas Scott, with the support of principle Carty, refused to allow the editorial to be published.

One of the essays that Colding and his fellow honor students, Judy Walker and Michael Bachelor, had already read in their AP English literature class was Henry David Thoreau's *On the Duty of Civil Disobedience.* Imagine these Black students whose great grandparents had been slaves, young men and women who had been called "Niggers" by their principal, who had been told they could not go to college, who had been told that the city needs more service workers and that their future was limited to service jobs, who had been aggressively controlled by campus police . . . imagine these bright, ambitious and energetic young men and women reading these words:

> How does it become a man to behave toward this American government today? I answer that he cannot without disgrace be associated with it. I cannot for an instant recognize that political organization as *my* government which is the *slave's* government also.[29]

Imagine these Detroit teens, growing up in the shadow of the automobile plants, encountering metaphor like this:

> If the injustice is part of the machine of government, let it go, let it go: perchance it will wear smooth—certainly the machine will wear out. If the injustice has a spring, or a pulley, or a rope, or a crank, exclusively for itself, then perhaps you may consider whether the remedy will not be worse than the evil; but if it is of such a nature that it requires you to be the agent of injustice to another, then, I say, break the law. Let your life be a counterfriction to stop

the machine. What I have to do is to see, at any rate, that I do not lend myself to the wrong which I condemn.[30]

What should their response be?

Colding, Walker, and Bachelor decided to organize, just like the workers in an automobile factory. They drew up a list of seven demands to present to the Board of Education Superintendent Samuel Brownell. These included the immediate removal of Principal Carty and the school's on-campus police officer, the hiring of qualified teachers, information on the academic standards at the school, and the creation of a student/faculty council to study school problems and propose solutions.

Samuel Brownell became Detroit's superintendent of schools in 1956, two years after the Supreme Court decision in the *Brown vs. the Board of Education* case, which ruled against separate public schools for Black and White students. Brownell publicly spoke in support of the ruling and had worked hard during his 10 years as superintendent to recruit Black teachers and administrators for the system, often upsetting the White community. Brownell had earlier served as the superintendent of the Grosse Pointe school system from 1927 to 1938. By 1966 one of the three public middle schools in Grosse Pointe had been named after him.[31]

Brownell immediately removed the police officer but allowed Carty to stay and promised to study the other issues in the future. This was not enough for the students. At 10:00 a.m. on April 20, 1966, Williams, Colding, Walker, and Bachelor, joined by 2,128 other students, walked out of the classroom demanding a better education. Only 183 students remained at their desks.

The students eventually prevailed. Brownell met with the Board of Education three days later and met all the student's demands, including having access to college preparatory classes. Williams, Colding, Walker, and Bachelor went on to graduate a year later. One month after they received their diplomas, the Virginia Park neighborhood, a few blocks from Northern High School, exploded in another, much larger protest.[32] Northern alumnus Billy Scott was there at the start of that week-long protest.

Billy Scott had no love for the Detroit Police Department. One of Mayor Cavanaugh's top priorities after his election in 1961 was to improve the relationship between the Department and the Black community. To do this he named George Edwards—a former mayoral candidate, justice on the Michigan Supreme Court, and a man trusted by the Black community—as police commissioner. Accepting the position as police commissioner was a step down for Justice Edwards. But he had a heart beating for both justice and compassion that can be heard in a speech to the Trade Union Leadership Council in April 1962. In that speech Edwards said, "My first job was to teach the police they didn't have a constitutional right to automatically beat up Negroes on arrest."[33]

Reforms by Edwards and his successor, Ray Girardin, were focused on increasing the professionalism within the department and on color-blind street policing. Edwards tripled the hours of human-relations training at the police academy and formally banned the use of racial slurs by police officers. Girardin took these reforms further and made major changes to the departmental citizens complaint bureau. This bureau was charged with receiving and investigating complaints of police misconduct. The complaints had to travel through many layers of administrative bureaucracy before finally landing on the commissioner's desk. Few ever survived the trip. Girardin placed the bureau directly under his office and moved its operations from police headquarters to the downtown YMCA. His goal was to ensure that "citizens would not have to walk into the lion's den to complain about the lions."[34]

These reforms seemed to work. In 1943 a three-day riot in the city had ended with Whites actually shooting Blacks on site in the Black neighborhoods of Black Bottom and Paradise Valley. Blood literally flowed in the streets. Michigan's governor, Harry Kelly, had declared martial law and requested the assistance of the U.S. Army. Over 50% of the 34 fatalities were the result of police or military force. Of the nearly 240 riots in the nation around that time, the Detroit riot was the most violent and the only one requiring federal assistance and martial law. By the 1960's, it was looking as if the city had turned itself around. In 1964 riots broke out in Harlem, Jersey City and Philadelphia. 1965 saw riots in the Watts district of Los Angeles. In the summer of 1966, there were riots in Cleveland, Chicago and San Francisco. A minor riot in Detroit in August of that year, the "Kercheval Incident" on the East Side, was brought under control without loss of life or DPD firing a single weapon. Scholars continue to debate whether it was the police department reforms or a well-timed rainstorm that deserves credit for the peaceful end of the Kercheval riot. But by the mid-1960s Detroit was seen as a model city for race-relations, the "City that Works." In May 1965, Mayor Cavanaugh secured a $213,000 grant from the U.S. Office of Economic Opportunity to institute an in-service program within the police department that focused on the civil rights of the public and ways to defuse situations between police and minority groups "without undue militancy, aggressiveness, hostility or prejudice."[35]

Unfortunately, the training did not effectively filter down to the street level. Most of the 1800 officers that completed the training wrote on their exit surveys that the training was useless. They gave the right answers in the classrooms, but once back on the beat they reverted to their old ways. Billy Scott's experiences demonstrated the disconnect between the ideals being promoted downtown and actual street-level policing.

For example, there was the time in 1965 when Scott was stopped for jaywalking across 12th street. In response to Scott's question of what he had done, a cop threw him against the car and referred to him as "boy." He was given a $10 ticket which Billy tore up in front of the officers and threw into the trash.

And then there was Billy's encounter with the Big Four. The Big Four was an initiative in response to requests from middle-class Black residents for more protection in high crime areas. Three plainclothes officers and a uniformed driver, armed with shotguns, teargas and gas masks, patrolled Black neighborhoods in a big car. The Big Four units were supposed to offer protection to Black residents, but usually they simply harassed Blacks in the poorer communities. One day Billy Scott and his two brothers were walking out of a store when they were stopped by one of the Big Four patrol cars and frisked for no reason. Scott vented his mounting anger by yelling at the police officers, "You can kiss my Black ass." When a crowd began to form, the police officers backed off.

And then there was the constant raiding of his father's club by the DPD—nine times during the year prior to the July rebellion. During the last raid, after being hit in the head by a police officer, Billy chose to "Uncle Tom my way out" and co-operate. That night he vowed that next time he would fight back, and even kill an officer if that was what it took.

And then there was the fatal shooting of a Black prostitute on July 1 on the corner of 12th and Hazelwood, two blocks from the club. Police said she was shot either by a pimp or a perspective customer, but word in the Black community was that her killer was an off-duty police officer.

Billy Scott had no love for the Detroit Police Department.

At about 3:44 a.m. on July 23, 1967, Billy Scott arrived at his father's club and saw a White cop swing a sledgehammer at the club's plate glass door. He watched as his father and his sister, Wilma, were aggressively pushed into a paddy wagon. "You don't have to treat them that way," Billy yelled. "They can walk. Let them walk."

"Proper," church-going Billy climbed on top of a car and yelled to the crowd: "Are we going to let these peckerwood mother f-----s come down here any time they want and mess us around?" "Hell no," came the reply.

Filled with rage, Billy went to an ally and found a bottle, intending to throw it at one of the officers. "Maybe kill one," he thought. Billy threw the bottle at a sergeant standing in front of the door and missed. Officers moved in, but recognizing they were outnumbered, quickly backed off. That bottle, thrown by William Scott III, was the first thrown in the conflict and became the match that ignited the rebellion.[36] As the paddy wagons and police cars drove off, others threw bottles, sticks, and bricks that smashed the windows of the police cars. The raid had turned into a riot.[37]

The next day *The Detroit News* published a front-page editorial for its predominately White, suburban audience. "It HAS happened here," the article began. "After years of success in preserving racial peace, and despite all that concerned community leadership—both Black and White—did to keep Detroit whole while it tackled its problems, it has happened here." It HAS happened here—in Detroit, in the 'City that Works.'

The rioters had no grounds for their unhappiness, according to the editorial. "The neighborhoods torn apart do not teem with unemployment. Times are not desperate in Detroit for people who want and can work and the rioters who rampaged were not confined to the unemployed." No mention of the fact that the new, efficient automotive plants were in the suburbs, miles from the neighborhoods where Blacks were allowed to live. The police, according to the *News* editorial, were beyond reproach. "Detroit's police, whatever old history may recall, have for some time functioned as a disciplined professional police force should conduct itself; they continued to so function all day yesterday and on into today's morning hours, even in the face of grave disorder and assault upon themselves. There was no 'police brutality.'" The writers of the editorial made clear what they thought of the rioters. "The toughs who transformed a crowd into a mob by smashing windows; the looters who exploited opportunity; all these can be called the product of past generations of injustice . . . But these mobsters, arsonists and looters were not fighting a civil rights battle." [38]

According to *The Detroit News,* William Scott III, "Billy," who was unable to get a job that summer so that he could return for a second year to Detroit Lutheran College, was a "tough." Charles Colding, Judy Walker and Michael Bachelor and other young men and women like them from Northern High School who were denied equal access to education had no grounds for their unhappiness. *The Detroit News* judged these young Americans to be "mobsters, arsonists and looters." They certainly "were not fighting a civil rights battle."

Six hours after Billy Scott threw that bottle, while turmoil continued to grow on the West side, my family quietly joined the congregation of The Fort as usual for the morning service. Some in the congregation undoubtedly already knew what was going on in the city, having learned the news by telephone from friends and family with connections to the west side. Others, like my family, undoubtedly did not. It was common after the service for members of the church to stand around and chat, catching up on one another's lives and other news of interest. I suspect our family first learned of the uprising sometime during or after that service.

Mayor Cavanagh did everything he could to delay the breaking of the story. He got in touch with the local news media and they agreed to sit on the story in order to give the city officials time to quell the disturbance. That afternoon the Detroit Tigers split a doubleheader at home against the New York Yankees. Tiger general manager Jim Campbell gave clear instructions to announcer Ray Lane: "You are not, I repeat not, under any circumstances, to refer to the smoke over the left-field fence."[39] Unfortunately Cavanagh's influence stopped at the river. It was the Canadian station, CKLW channel 9 out of Windsor that broke the story at 2:00 p.m. The Detroit TV stations began their coverage a few hours later.

In April 1861, the Society women of Charleston, S.C. gathered on The Battery dressed in their finery to watch the Confederate attack on the Union held Fort Sumter. In January 1991, the world watched on CNN as the American led coalition began Operation Desert Shield in response to Saddam Hussein's invasion of Kuwait. In July 1967, my family watched the Rebellion on our black-and-white Motorola TV.

I will forever remember those black-and-white television images of fires. I had seen firemen do their work. One Friday night while we were visiting Grandma in Ludington a large souvenir shop, "Fort Ludington" on Ludington Avenue, a place that looked like a real fort and sold cheap wooden trinkets with the word "Ludington" stamped on them, was gutted by fire. We walked the six blocks from Grandma's house to Fort Ludington several times that weekend to watch the progress of the firefighters. Another time, as we were driving to The Fort on a Sunday morning, we observed firefighters finishing their work at a bar on Mack Avenue in Grosse Pointe Farms that had been totally destroyed by a fire caused by a cigarette.

But this was different. Day after day, throughout the week, images of blazing and smoldering buildings dominated the television screen. Streets ordinarily filled with automobiles now served as concrete trenches for fire hoses. Three firefighters holding a single fire hose. Always three. Always at a distance from the camera, a dark and shadowy silhouette. A helpless Trinity holding hoses that sprayed water into the burning buildings, hoping at best to keep the fires from spreading. Fire trucks. Buildings in flames with no firefighters to put them out. The same images, over and over again. My father said the television stations were showing the same fires from Sunday all week to keep interest.

And smoke. Television images of smoke. Smoke rising from the streets. Aerial images of smoke rising from the city. A messy, dirty cloud. Dirtier and uglier than the mushroom clouds of Hiroshima and Nagasaki. We could smell the smoke as we saw it rise up from burning buildings on our TV screen. A heavy, dirty stench chocking out what little oxygen remained in the humid July air. A disgusting odor polluting the normally fresh lakeside air of the five Pointes, twenty miles away.

And images of looters. Young Black men walking into stores in broad daylight and taking things. Groceries. Shoes. I couldn't imagine

43

someone just walking through a store window and taking something. In my naïve, Calvinist trained mind where the Ten Commandments were read every Sunday morning at The Fort, this was stealing. And it was the Black people who were doing the stealing. I don't remember ever seeing a White looter, nor are there any on the YouTube videos of the incident that are available today.

I had no idea where 12th Street and Clairmont was. Our family made occasional trips to downtown Detroit, especially Cobo Hall and Arena. I had taken school trips downtown by chartered bus to children's programs at the Ford Auditorium, often using surface streets such as Jefferson and Charlevoix. I had witnessed firsthand the poverty of Detroit's ghettos, which were synonymous in my mind with the Black communities. The storefronts on Twelfth Street I saw on TV looked just like the storefronts on Mack Avenue. They had the same display windows. They stood on the edge of the sidewalk, no parking lot, yard, or grass separating the two. The similarity of Twelfth Street and the more familiar Mack Avenue, with the former lying completely in ruins, made the whole experience very real to me. I was not scared. I was stunned, emotionless, numb.

My vocabulary was enriched throughout the week. In addition to learning about "looting," I learned what a "blind pig" was. Apparently, this was a term unique to the Detroit dialect of the English language, as my parents did not know what it was either. My innocent mind discovered that week that bars were supposed to close at certain times, something I didn't know. Sometimes bartenders would push the limits and serve customers after the legal closing time. When they did so, it was called a "blind pig." I think I got the idea somehow that Detroit was the only place where this happened, that everywhere else bartenders followed the law. I knew nothing about liquor licenses or about any

44

connection between one's race and the ability to get such a license. What I learned was that Black people on 12th Street were drinking after closing time. They were violating the law.

I learned about something called "race riots." I had never heard of such a thing. We certainly didn't have them in Grand Rapids or Kalamazoo.[40] I learned that week that this was the worst race riot in Detroit in 24 years. I knew nothing about the Kerchival incident, or of rioting in other large cities across the country. But in 1943, long before I was born, Detroit had a race riot. Now it was experiencing another. I came to the logical conclusion that race riots were a regular and even normal thing in Detroit, and that we had been fortunate to go so long without having had one. Children can be very naive.

President Johnson gave his assessment of what was going on in Detroit, an assessment that made sense complete sense to my young mind, in his address to the nation on Thursday of that week:

> First, let there be no mistake about it-the looting, arson, plunder, and pillage which have occurred are not part of the civil rights protest. There is no American right to loot stores, or to burn buildings, or to fire rifles from the rooftops. That is crime—and crime must be dealt with forcefully, and swiftly, and certainly— under law.

I can still hear that Southern drawl of the President pronouncing the verdict: Crime.

There is an ongoing debate as to whether the events in Detroit that week in July should be referred to as a "riot," a "rebellion," or a "revolution. The editorial board of The *Detroit Free Press* published an editorial on Thursday of that week that said:

One thing the riots were not. They were not a massive Negro uprising against White people. There was little hatred in the Sunday outbreak. There were Negro and White looters and snipers fought by Negro and White policemen and soldiers. It wasn't basically race against race. This needs to be emphasized because some terms used to describe what happened—Negro riots, ghetto uprising, Negro rebellion—don't really describe what occurred in Detroit.[41]

According to the *Detroit Free Press,* it wasn't race against race. So what was it? There was certainly a racial component to it. But there was an economic one as well. As Dr. Rita Fields points out, the riot was also an expression of the frustration of those on the lowest rungs of the economic ladder, White or Black.[42] Fewer than ten percent of the 500,000 African Americans living in the city were involved, while Caucasians who were not poor began arriving from as many as four states in their cars and filled them up with loot.[43] One writer suggests that while "most of the press insisted on calling the 1967 experience a race riot . . . the facts are that the 1967 Detroit disorder was one of the most integrated events in recent history."[44]

The *Free Press* itself had contributed to the confusion earlier in the week in its original reporting of the riot:

> Gov. Romney called in the National Guard and clamped a state of emergency on Detroit Sunday night in an attempt to quell spreading Negro-sniping, burning and looting that broke out on the Twelfth and Clairmount area on the city's West Side. . . After 17 hours of rampage by Negroes, triggered by an early-morning police raid on an illegal after-hours liquor spot, the area was a shambles [sic] of shattered and demolished stores and blazing buildings. . .

> The scene in the Twelfth and Clairmount area was one of complete pandemonium as gangs of Negroes looted and burned at random.

The outbreak was the first of its kind in Detroit since last August, when Negroes touched off three nights of violence in the Kircheval and Pennsylvania area on the East Side. Unlike the East Side area, which is predominately residential with mixed Negro and White residents, Twelfth is almost entirely a Negro area.

The spark that touched off the festering Negro resentment against White store owners and police was a 3:45 a.m. raid by Livernios Station officers at a blind pig at 9215 Twelfth. . .

A Crowd of about 200 Negroes formed across the street as police began to load 83 prisoners into vans. The crowd began to yell obscenities at police and to hurl bottles.

Negroes who witnessed the raid claimed police manhandled the prisoners.[45]

The first three looters killed were White, including the first looter to die, Walter Grzunka. He was sitting on the porch Sunday evening watching some of his neighbors walk by with their booty and decided to get some for himself. At The Temple Market he encountered a young Black man who handed him a bag of loot. He carried it across the street and gave it to some of his friends and went back for more. On his third trip he was fatally shot by the store's owner, 30-year-old Hamid Audish Yacoub, from his 1965 Ford Mustang. In Grzunka's pockets were seven cigars, four packs of tobacco, and nine pairs of shoelaces.[46] The *Free Press* noted that Grzunka was shot by an unknown person at Temple Market, that he was pronounced dead at General Hospital, and his address. The paper did not report that Grzunka was White. The looters were both Black and White, but the television cameras never filmed a White looter.

A ten-year-old child looks to his parents for guidance in dealing with new experiences such as this, and I was no exception. It quickly became clear to me that this was something serious. Like everyone else in metropolitan Detroit, my parents were glued to the television set those first few hours, shocked as they watched the live footage of the riots on our television set. After the shock came disbelief. Then a paralyzing fear. We were still relatively new to Detroit, and this was something far beyond the experiences of my mother who came from the small town of Ludington and my father who grew up among the Dutch in Grand Rapids.

A man of character and integrity will do what he must to protect his family, and my dad was that kind of man. As the "head of the house" in those pre-feminism days, his first concern was for the wellbeing and protection of our family. I was the oldest at 10, followed by my two sisters, ages 8 and 3, and my brother who at just over a year was still a baby. Dad began talking about how to get us all out of Detroit. The obvious solution was to send us to the west side of the state, to my grandparents' cottage on Gun Lake to stay with them. Dad's plan was to stay behind to work, and probably keep an eye on the house. The problem was that in order to get there, we would have to take the Edsel Ford freeway (I-94) downtown to the John C. Lodge freeway (US 10). The Lodge freeway would take us right through the riot area. Another option was to take Eight Mile Road across town and meet the Lodge freeway in Southfield. My mother was not comfortable with either route. I never understood why we couldn't take I-94 northeast to Port Huron and then drive across the state from there. I suspect the truth is that my mother did not want to make that drive alone with the four children. Nor did she want her family to be separated during this time of crisis.

Another family from The Fort, Jack and Lea Nyenhuis, did make the journey across Eight Mile road. They were not in church that Sunday morning as they were camping at Holland State Park. When they learned about the unrest sometime before their return to the Detroit metropolitan area, they chose to take the Eight Mile Road route to their home in Grosse Pointe Park. As they were driving along Eight Mile Road with their three daughters (one of whom was my classmate), they saw looters with shotguns. Like my Dad, their main concern was for the safety of the family. Rather than continuing to their home, they chose to spend the evening in Bloomfield Hills with friends.

So how does a man keep his family safe? Ordinarily he relies on the police department to fulfill this responsibility, and like the other four Grosse Pointes, the Woods had its own police force. But as the week progressed and the National Guard called in with federal troops being discussed to augment the force, the ordinary sense of safety quickly disappears. How does a man recapture that sense of safety? With a gun.

This is long before the days of the national discussion about the Second Amendment. Long before the time when the National Rifle Association was a major political power. In my experience, ordinary middle-class people like us didn't have handguns for protection. They had shotguns and rifles for hunting. My Dad had a 12-gauge and a 20-gauge shotgun for that purpose. That week he loaded both guns and kept them standing upright in the corner of his bedroom every night while he slept—or tried to sleep.

Under ordinarily circumstances we rarely saw a Black person in our neighborhood. The one exception was the maids or "cleaning women" as my mother would call them. We never had a maid, but some of our neighbors did. The week of the riots none of them came to work. My father thought there was no need for a Black person to be in Grosse

Pointe during such turmoil and said if he saw one on his property, he would shoot first and ask questions later. Fortunately, he never had to make that call. But, like the looting on Twelfth Street, shooting a Black person on our property violated one of those Ten Commandments read every Sunday morning at The Fort, and was simply not right in my young mind. I know for my Dad this was also a challenge for his faith. Where do you aim? He eventually concluded that he would aim for the intruder's legs first. But it was clear in my Dad's mind that he would do whatever it took to keep his family safe. And so, here was my Dad, a Grosse Pointe Hillbilly behaving in the tradition of Jed Clampett, with a loaded shotgun. The question of whether this was right or wrong has troubled me ever since. As I grew older and after serving a career in the military, I have come to understand that war requires its participants to make some very difficult choices. And this was a war. The presence of army troops later in the week made that quite clear.

Sometime after the riots were over, my father bought a small pistol to use for target practice. When he went to register the gun, the clerk assisting him asked why he did not purchase a larger weapon. His response was, "I don't want to shoot anyone! This is just for target practice." Apparently, there was a large increase in the sale of handguns following the rebellion, and most of them were not purchased with the intent of being aimed at a can on a stump somewhere in the woods. My Dad always kept the pistol locked in a safe place.

My parents, like most Grosse Pointers, were conservative and strong Republicans. So when the elected officials began to appear on the television set, I got a good lesson in politics, Republican style. Mayor Cavanagh was a Democrat and unable to control the city with his liberal policies. So he called Michigan's Governor George Romney, a

Republican, to come in and save the day. Romney, according to this version of the story, was a good guy and strong leader. He called in the National Guard to clean up the mess made by Cavanaugh. But President Johnson, another soft Democrat, was not willing to send in federal troops immediately. So obviously, it was Cavanaugh's ineptitude in the first place and Johnson's unwillingness to send in federal troops that resulted in the riots continuing nearly a full week before being brought under control.

Like everyone in the Detroit area, my parents were frustrated and angry at how long it took to get the disturbance under control. My political education, however, lacked a few relevant details. I didn't learn the fact that Cavanaugh, in consultation with Negro leaders, requested the assistance of both the State Police and National Guard from Romney. Or the fact that the Michigan Governor, father of the 2012 Republican nominee for the White House, Mitt Romney, had his own eye on a potential run for the Presidency and was concerned with presenting an image of a strong leader as he dealt with the situation in Detroit. Or the fact that federal troops were not used to end any of the recent riots including the 1964 riots in Harlem, Jersey City and Philadelphia, the 1965 riots Watts, or the 1966 riots in Cleveland, Chicago and San Francisco.[47] Or the fact that neither Romney nor Johnson wanted to be responsible for television images of a predominately White federal force aiming weapons at a predominately Black target.[48] Or the fact that both the President and Romney had different legal concerns about the precise wording of the Governor's request for federal troops. Romney's advisors encouraged him to avoid any terminology that could be used by insurance companies to avoid paying for damages in the affected areas; Johnson's advisors were saying that such language was required by the governor before any federal intervention could be legally given.[49] These facts were either unknown or of little concern to those of us in Detroit and Grosse Pointe. What we saw was a reenactment of Nero's Rome: the politicians fiddled while Detroit burned.[50]

Johnson finally signed the order at 11:58 p.m. Monday night to send in the federal troops, based in part on information he received from FBI Director J. Edgar Hoover who informed the President that a similar situation was likely to ignite in Harlem within an hour.[51] His televised remarks to the nation were clearly a political jab against Romney:

> I am sure the American people will realize that I take this action with the greatest regret—and only because of the clear, unmistakable, and undisputed evidence that Governor Romney of Michigan and the local officials in Detroit have been unable to bring the situation under control. Law enforcement is a local matter. It is the responsibility of local officials and the Governors of the respective States. The Federal Government should not intervene - except in the most extraordinary circumstances. The fact of the matter, however, is that law and order have broken down in Detroit, Michigan.[52]

U.S. Army troops of the 82nd and 101st Airborne Units immediately began flooding in from Selfridge Air Base in Mount Clemons, where they had gathered awaiting the President's order. That night Detroit became the only city in the nation to be occupied by federal troops twice (1943 and 1967).

The President was now in charge, and he faced a new challenge in addition to the looting and fires: sniper fire. Sixteen reports of sniper fire on the police, firefighters and guardsmen were recorded Monday night between 9:00 and 10:00—while Johnson and Romney tried to settle their differences. Things deteriorated from there. By midnight two police precincts, two command posts, and five fire stations were under attack by snipers. How many of the snipers were Vietnam War veterans, now using the skills they learned for combat training against the police and guardsmen? The historical record is unclear. What is clear is that Johnson now had two wars on his hands.

Johnson's second war became very real to me that week. Helicopters from Selfridge began flying overhead. One day, while riding my one-speed Murray bike on the pedestrian overpass across I-94 three blocks from our house, I stopped at the top of that bridge and watched the traffic below: tanks and army trucks loaded with troops were headed toward downtown Detroit. A parade of green that gave me an eerie sense of safety and puzzlement. In my young life I had never seen so many tanks and army trucks. What were they doing here? Helicopters, tanks and army trucks belong in Vietnam, not Detroit. How do I make sense of all this?

The first paragraph of the headline article in the Detroit News on Wednesday was filled with military language and imagery from Vietnam: "Negro snipers turned 140 square blocks north of West Grand Boulevard into a bloody battlefield for three hours last night, temporarily routing police and national guardsmen." Below the fold was a more graphic article, entitled "Snipers vs. Machine Guns: Guerrilla War Rips 12th."

> Backed by tanks and armed personnel carriers, national guardsmen and police last night and early today fought house-to-house war on 12th Street. The scene was incredible.
>
> It was as though the Viet Cong had infiltrated the riot-blacked streets.
>
> Snipers in what sounded like at least two dozen locations snapped off rounds as police and riflemen slid past the dingy houses.
>
> They were answered by quick volleys of M-1 carbines, blasts from machine guns and bursts from sub-machine guns.

Then there was the clanking whine of a tank or a personnel carrier.

A 50-caliber machine gun roared in 30-second bursts, sweeping a roof, building or alley. Silence for a second, broken only by the soft sounds of moving troops.[53]

It was just over twelve miles from my home in Grosse Pointe Woods to Virginia Park, where Billy Scott III threw his bottle and started the uprising. The helicopters, tanks, and trucks filled with troops assured me that I was safe. But things were more intense for those who lived in Grosse Pointe Park, near The Fort. By the time President Johnson appeared on national television at midnight on Monday, July 24, the rioting had moved to the East Side. Three hours before the President announced, "Law and order have broken down in Detroit, Michigan," a report came in of sniper fire on the corner of Charlevoix and Hillger, where a Guardsman had been shot; eighteen minutes later there was a second report of a Guardsman shot (possibly the same one). The Fort was less than 2 miles from this area; two miles from the battlefront. By 10:30 p.m., the sniper fire was so heavy that the State Police pulled out of the area.[54] This was the exact time that President Johnson, according to his speech later that evening, made the decision to deploy federal troops.

At approximately 10:30 this evening, Mr. Vance and General Throckmorton reported to me by telephone that it was the then unanimous opinion of all the state and federal officials who were in consultation—including Governor Romney, Mr. Vance, General Throckmorton, the mayor, and others—that the situation had developed in such a way in the few intervening hours as to make the use of federal troops to augment the police and Michigan National Guard imperative. They described the situation in considerable detail, including the violence and deaths that had occurred in the past few hours, and submitted as the unanimous judgment of all concerned that the situation was totally beyond the control of the local authorities.[55]

The "violence and deaths that had occurred in the past few hours" occurred that evening on the east side of the city. It was the rioting on the east side of the city, two miles from the exclusive (and White) suburb of Grosse Pointe, that was now out of control and required President Johnson's authorizing the use of federal troops. The Fort stood just two miles from the battlefront, a highly visible yet probably unnoticed symbol of God's presence amidst the chaos.

A number of people gathered in front of Lou's Party Store on Lakepointe and Charlevoix that evening, two blocks from The Fort. The sun sets late in Michigan in July, somewhere around 10 p.m. The small crowd of Grosse Pointers, which included a number of members from The Fort, looked down the deserted Charlevoix Avenue and saw the rising smoke in the distance. Members of the church reported hearing gunfire from their homes. Jack Nyenhuis, who by this time had returned from Bloomfield Hills to his home in Grosse Pointe, tells of the local policeman stopping in front of his house as he sat on the front porch and telling him to go inside for his own safety.[56]

Incredibly, US Army General John Throckmorton, who was now commander of both the federal and state troops, gave the order that the federal troops would only patrol east of Woodward Avenue, leaving the hardest hit sections on the west side to the exhausted state troops and state and local police forces. He set up a military checkpoint at the intersection of Altar and Mack, a bunker three blocks from The Fort. The Michigan Bell Telephone building on the Detroit side of Mack Avenue where it intersects with Cadieux Road was the tallest building in the area. It became a makeshift watchtower. I still remember the armed soldiers on the flat roof of the building, waving at the passers-by. The police and state troopers would have to deal with the West Side. President Johnson's federal troops would make sure that White, affluent Grosse Pointe would be kept safe from any invasion.

*Michigan may geographically be one of America's most northern states, but spiritually it is one of its most southern."*

-Charlie LeDuff[57]

*"African Americans degrade neighborhoods—making them less clean, less safe, less desirable, and less valuable."*

-Southern Whites[58]

# Chapter 3

# Houses for Autoworkers

Before Dirk Eppinga left the Netherlands for America sometime around 1910, his parents made him visit the pastor. During that visit the minister explained to him that there were two churches in America serving Dutch people, one called the Reformed Church and the other called the Christian Reformed Church. "You must by no means join the Reformed, you must join the Christian Reformed," the pastor insisted.[59] The pastor's guidance was driven by events in the ecclesiastical world of the Netherlands beginning in 1834 when a group known as the *Afgescheiden,* "Separatists," left the state-run Dutch Reformed Church and formed a more conservative church. The Reformed Church, the full name of which was The Reformed Church *in America* (italics mine), was the New World equivalent to the Dutch Reformed Church. The *Christian* (italics mine) Reformed Church was the church of the *Afgescheidenen.* The Eppingas were from the northern part of the Netherlands where the majority of the *Afgescheidenen* lived, so because of their conservative beliefs they were *Afgescheidenen.*

Eppinga's pastor most likely never mentioned the Ku Klux Klan or Jim Crow. He had no idea that the church Eppinga would help establish in America would eventually be shaped more by the struggle against these two demonic threats than by Dutch theological disputes.

Dirk immigrated to America and discovered there was a huge demand in Detroit for carpenters, his chosen trade. Henry Ford's offer of five dollar a day wages was drawing thousands of factory workers into the city, and there was a pressing need for houses. Eppinga joined with a man named

59

Hickey, formed the Hickey and Eppinga Construction Company, and started building houses. Thousands of houses. Not elaborate houses meant for the wealthy of Grosse Pointe. They built functional family homes for blue-collar workers. The center and largest room of a Hickey and Eppinga house was the dining room, built to accommodate a table large enough to seat the entire family and could be extended to provide seating for extended family on Sundays and other guests during the week.

Dickey & Eppinga Construction Company, co-owners Hickey on left and Dirk Eppinga on right (in suits). Courtesy of Rev. Jacob Eppinga

The table usually had a matching hutch or buffet where the treasured china could be stored. Behind the dining room was the kitchen, small by modern standards. No dishwasher. Limited counter space as there was no need to display the more modern electric treasures like toasters and mixers, and certainly not microwave ovens. Enough room to prepare the meal and stack the dishes afterward—dirty dishes on one side and clean on the other, with the sink in the middle, a domestic assembly line allowing the after-dinner chore to be completed efficiently. Between the dining room and the street was the living room. Centered on one wall facing the street was the largest window of the entire house, allowing the family to keep an eye on what the neighbors were doing. The outer wall perpendicular to the large window often had a fireplace which was used to create a cozy and inviting atmosphere for the family to gather in during long winter evenings before the advent of television. The living room was smaller than the dining room. A couch, one or two easy chairs, a couple of end tables beneath reading lamps and perhaps a coffee table were all the furnishings the room could hold. After dinner the children had the choice of sitting at the dining room table or lying on the living room rug that covered the hardwood floor to do their homework. In front of the living room and on the other side of the picture window was a large, open front porch. This served as a second living room in the summer, a place where neighbors passing by on the sidewalk could be greeted and invited up to share a glass of lemonade or a beer. A master bedroom—not a suite, like is so common today, but a relatively small bedroom—and a bathroom completed the main floor plan. Upstairs were the rest of the bedrooms where the children slept. Each of the second-floor bedrooms was just a fraction of a room, as the slanted ceiling required anyone over three feet tall to lean to one side. The bedroom in the front often boasted a dormer, which allowed for more space. Hickey and Eppinga homes were designed to foster social interaction, not privacy.

The families who purchased Hickey and Eppinga homes generally needed financing. Mortgages were not nearly as easy to obtain as they are today. The buyer generally needed a 50% down payment. He was required to pay only the interest on the note during the life of the loan, usually 5 years. When the note came due, he was required to pay back the entire principle, which sometimes required refinancing. The only Detroiters who could come up with such a large down payment were members of the older immigrant communities, primarily the Germans and Irish. Their move to these newer and more spacious bungalows opened up the smaller, older homes near the factories for more recent White immigrants from Poland, Hungary, and Russia as well as emigrating White Southerners. Few if any Hickey and Eppinga houses were purchased by African Americans.

The decade during which Eppinga immigrated from the Netherlands to Detroit also saw the rise in Black migration to the city. In 1910 the Black population of the city was just over one percent, 5,741 out of a total population of 465,766.[60] By 1919 there were 11,000 Negros working in the city's factories, primarily in the foundries and steel plants that required heavy labor in unbearably hot environments.[61] At the beginning of the decade, Blacks lived peacefully alongside Whites throughout the city and poor Whites lived in the predominately Black neighborhoods of Black Bottom and Paradise Valley. With Ford's offer of $5 a day wages and the start of the Great Migration, everything changed. The movement of Blacks from the Deep South and Whites from the Appalachian states of Kentucky, Tennessee, and West Virginia essentially turned Detroit into a Southern town. By 1948 there were nearly a half million Southerners in Detroit, a quarter of the city's population.[62]

Southern Whites believed that "African Americans degraded neighborhoods—making them less clean, less safe, less desirable, and less valuable."[63] As many as eight trainloads of African Americans arrived in the city every day, and they all needed a place to stay. Their housing opportunities were limited to the Black neighborhoods of Black Bottom and Paradise Valley, as well as to a few Black "colonies" located close to the city center. These communities became increasingly crowded. Family housing was provided by single and multi-family tenements, with multiple families crowding into each unit. Single men were billeted in boarding houses. In order to increase revenue and serve their many customers, boarding house owners developed a practice known as "hot sheets," renting a room for eight hours allowing factory workers time for sleep between shifts. Rents in the Black neighborhoods were high. City services, including garbage collection and law enforcement, were insufficient to keep up with the overpopulation. Rats ran freely in the streets. Poverty, overcrowding, and inadequate police protection created the perfect storm for the breeding of crime. This only served to reinforce the Southern Whites claim that African Americans degraded neighborhoods.

Meanwhile Dutch immigration from the Netherlands and Dutch American migration from West Michigan to Detroit during the decade between 1910 and 1920 nearly tripled the Dutch speaking population of the city.[64] Many of the immigrants from the Netherlands received the same guidance from their ministers as had Dirk Eppinga: "You must by no means join the Reformed, you must join the Christian Reformed." Those who came from Christian Reformed churches in Holland and Grand Rapids Michigan had a similar desire to be a part of a Christian Reformed Church. This kind of denominational loyalty and minute theological distinctions must seem quaint to the modern reader. For the Dutch in the early 20th century these were very real concerns, often discussed in great detail and with deeply felt emotion. Unfortunately for the *Afgescheidenen* from the Netherlands and the Christian Reformed people from the other side of the state, the only church in Detroit that offered morning and evening services in the Dutch language was a

Reformed Church. It went by the creative name of "First Reformed Church."

As the population of the city grew, so did the need for houses. Six days a week, week after week, Dirk built Detroit houses. And, week after week Dirk rested on the seventh day, following the example of his God. A proper Sabbath Day for this house builder required attendance at the house of the Lord, the church, and so Dirk, along with the other *Afgescheidenen* and Christian Reformed people, attended services at the First Reformed Church.

This Dutch speaking Detroit church was theologically and culturally a good fit for Dirk and the other immigrants. The preaching and structure of the services were thoroughly Calvinistic. The traditional Dutch Reformed taboos—what were known as "worldly amusements"—were strictly forbidden. Three sins qualified as worldly amusements: dancing, card playing and theater attendance. Dancing was seen as leading to sexual arousal. Card playing was linked to gambling, although only card games using poker cards found in casinos were forbidden. Games like "Rook" and "Dutch Blitz," which also used cards, were acceptable. Theater attendance was also linked to the potential for sexual arousal. Movies like *Gone with the Wind* featured beautiful women—and dancing. "What if Jesus returned and found you in a theater?" was the question often asked in defense of the restriction. Unlike many American Protestant churches of the day, alcohol consumption was permitted in moderation, and smoking—especially cigars—was a common practice by the men.

But in spite of all these theological, cultural and social similarities, the fact was that First Reformed Church was affiliated with the Reformed Church of America and that meant it was "liberal." To be liberal was the worst possible judgment that could be placed on a church.

Dirk and the others from his background willingly participated in the services and fellowship of First Reformed, but they refused to allow their membership papers to be transferred to this Detroit congregation. When asked to join, they would respond, "We can't join that, we have to join a Christian Reformed Church."

It is unlikely that anyone from First Reformed Church was surprised when, on January 11, 1914, thirteen Christian Reformed people met together to form their own congregation. For $25 they rented a small chapel attached to the much larger Clinton Street Baptist Church on the corner of Clinton Street and Joseph Campau. Reverend J. R. Brink was invited to come from Grand Rapids and lead the people in worship. Five months later, on June 11, the new congregation held its first service in the Baptist chapel as an organized Christian Reformed Church and was allowed to hold memberships. Dirk Eppinga, who was only a baptized member in the Netherlands, officially joined the church by making Profession of Faith. Making Profession of Faith was, and still is, an important milestone in any CRC member's life. It is a ceremony where he or she affirms their baptism and becomes a full church member.

Two issues consumed the new congregation's energies during the early years. The first was language. Eppinga's new church, like First Reformed, was a Dutch church. The first two services, held on the morning and evening of January 11, 1914, were held in the "Holland language." According to the church's Fiftieth Anniversary Book, "The service of the Lord in their own language was very precious to our Holland brethren."[65] Singing the familiar words of the Psalms, hearing the readings from the *StatenBijbel* (published in 1637, sixteen years after the King James Version was published in English) and hearing sermons in the mother tongue, were deeply comforting to their displaced souls.

There was a deeper reason for clinging to the Dutch language, and that was the fear of Americanization. While the Dutch had a positive view of America as a place of freedom and hope, they had a deep fear of Americanization. The Dutch were White, but they were not Anglo-Saxon. They had their own traditions and their own beloved Reformed faith, which could easily be lost forever in this new, large country that rose out of the British Empire. The Dutch language combined with the Reformed faith served as a barrier, a solid wall that separated them from the rest of Americans.

But from the beginning there were those who wanted services in English. The First Reformed Church had already held afternoon English services for several years in addition to the morning and evening Dutch services. By November 1915—before the second anniversary of the fledging young church and more than two years before the congregation was able to secure the services of its own full-time pastor—the evening service had been changed to English. It was the young people of the church who led the way, teaching the older generation how to sing the Psalms in English.

The "war to end all wars" going on in Europe intensified the language struggle. Americans had a difficult time distinguishing between the English word "Dutch" and the German word *Deutsch* (the German word for "German"). Christian Reformed people did not want to be identified with the *Deutsch*, the Germans, who were America's enemies. The similarity between the Dutch and German languages added to the confusion. Throughout the denomination, the church's members fully supported the war. They sent their young men off to battle, where they attended military chapels and were immersed in American ways. These Christian Reformed GIs came back identifying themselves as Americans, and church members began to see America rather than the Netherlands as their land.

The desire to hang on to the ethnic and religious traditions and the belief that they could best be expressed in the mother tongue was not unique to the Dutch. Other immigrant communities throughout Detroit and other American cities during this time period faced the same struggle. German Lutherans established what is today known as Historic Trinity Lutheran Church, "the Mother Church of Detroit Lutheranism," in 1850.[66] In 1904 the first Hungarian Reformed Church was established in the Delray neighborhood in the southwestern part of the city.[67] In 1915, one year after the Dutch established The Fort, Holy Trinity Orthodox Church was established in what was known as the "Russian Colony," a neighborhood now surrounded by Interstate 75 and the Davison Freeway.[68] Ethnic-religious immigrant communities wishing to maintain their traditions, their faith, and their language were a major feature of the city.

The second challenge the young Dutch congregation faced helped bring a final resolution to the language issue. As their numbers continued to increase during that decade of explosive growth in the Motor City, the members realized they needed a building of their own. Their first move, from the Baptist Chapel to a building on Chene Street, was made on January 18, 1916. The building was purchased from the Zion Reformed Church, a German-speaking congregation, for $13,000. For a number of months services were held in three languages. Morning and evening Dutch and English services alternated with services in German. When the Germans finally vacated the building (presumably to occupy a new building of their own), the members of The Fort decided to hold four services each Sunday, two in Dutch and two in English.

Various buildings that served as worship sites for the First Christian Reformed Church. Photo courtesy of First Christian Reformed Church of Detroit.

By 1923 the congregation had outgrown the Chene Street building, so in September of that year they sold the building and began worshipping in the school of St. Paul's Lutheran Church. In November they purchased two lots at the present site on the eastern edge of the city, and broke ground for a new 400-seat sanctuary. By February 4 and 5, 1925, the congregation was able to celebrate the dedication of a new, $61,400 building. The Fort became the first Dutch church to leave the old Belgian-Dutch neighborhood.[69] This geographic transition and the desire for all the congregational members to worship together were likely important factors in making the final change to English. With deep sadness and some fear, the older members yielded to the needs of the younger people who did not understand the "Holland language," and the Dutch services were discontinued.[70] The first wall protecting the church's members from the frightening influences of the surrounding city was removed. From then on, all services were held in English.

Meanwhile Dirk Eppinga continued building houses and selling them at a fair price to the residents of the growing city, using the proceeds to support his growing family and his beloved church. The focus of this Dutch-speaking carpenter was almost certainly not on issues of racial prejudice. Quality construction would have been foremost in his mind. The quality of his work was an expression of his religious piety, summed up in the verse from the Dutch Bible, *Hetzij  dat gij iets anders doet, doet het al ter ere Gods* ("Whatsoever ye do, do all to the glory of God," I Corinthians 10:31 KJV).

Naturally, the buyers of the quality Hickey and Eppinga homes on Detroit's East Side wanted to protect their investment. Many were concerned that the Southern Whites were right, that "African Americans degraded neighborhoods—making them less clean, less safe, less desirable, and less valuable." But keeping Black residents from settling in the developing neighborhoods was not easy. In 1917, three years after the founding of Dirk Eppinga's new church, the Supreme Court of the United States ruled in the case of *Buchanan v. Warley* that city governments were prohibited from enforcing segregation laws. No longer able to rely on the force of law, homeowners had to develop new ways to protect their investment. One way was through violence. On five different occasions during the spring and summer of 1925 White mobs drove an African American family out of a White neighborhood where they had purchased a house. Another way to protect property values was through the development of restrictive covenants or deeds that all residents of a given neighborhood agreed to follow. These covenants included stipulations such as prohibiting commercial activity, forbidding construction of multiple-residence homes and dividing of single-family homes into rental units. They almost always prohibited the selling of houses to people from racial or ethnic minority groups. Over 80 percent of the new communities outside Grand Boulevard had restrictive deeds that excluded Blacks. [71]

The realtors were more than willing to support segregation as a way to maintain property values. The National Association of Real Estate Boards adopted a code of ethics in 1924 that included the following words:

> A realtor should never be instrumental in introducing into a neighborhood. . . members of any race or nationality . . . whose presence will clearly be detrimental to property values in that neighborhood.[72]

With the adoption of this code realtors were ethically required to not assist any Blacks who wanted to move to a White neighborhood. The National Association of Real Estate Boards' code of ethics effectively institutionalized segregation. Fifteen years later realtors would institute similar policies in Grosse Pointe to enforce segregation.

One Black man who was able to bypass the realtors and purchase a Hickey and Eppinga style house[73] was Dr. Ossian Sweet. Sweet purchased the home at 2905 Garland Street from the original owner in the summer of 1925 for $18,500, the fifth African American family to move into a White neighborhood that spring and summer. He experienced the same welcome as the others: hundreds of Whites gathered around his new home, throwing rocks, breaking windows, shooting at those inside, and threatening to burn the houses down.

The KKK was especially strong in Detroit in the mid-1920s. Burning crosses and men marching in white hoods were a common sight. In 1924 an anti-Catholic proposal to outlaw parochial schools in the state of Michigan was defeated. In September of that same year the KKK candidate for mayor won the primary vote. It was only after 17,000 votes were ruled invalid based on a technicality that his opponent was declared the winner.[74] On July 11 the following year 10,000 Klansmen gathered for a rally on West Fort Street, where a speaker surrounded by fiery crosses called for laws allowing Negroes to live in only certain sections of the city.[75] The next day a paid announcement appeared in *The Detroit Free Press*:

> To maintain the high standard of the residential district between Jefferson and Mack Avenues, a meeting has been called by the Waterworks Improvement Association for Thursday night in the Howe School Auditorium. Men and women of the district, which includes Cadillac, Hurburt, Garland, St. Clair, and Harding Avenues, are asked to attend in self-defense.

Seven hundred people attended the meeting and discussed the rumor that a Black family, the Sweets, had purchased the house at 2905

Garland. "Where the nigger shows his head, the White man must shoot," yelled the speaker. The crowd cheered.[76]

On September 8th, Dr. Sweet, fully aware of the danger, moved his family into their new house. "I have to die like a man or live like a coward," he said to his brother. Included in his belongings were nine guns and enough ammunition for all of them. Dr. Sweet notified the Detroit police and asked for protection. The evening passed without incident.[77]

The next night as Mrs. Sweet was preparing dinner someone looked out the window and exclaimed, "My God, look at the people!" An angry crowd had gathered outside the home.

Around eight o'clock Sweet's brother and a friend arrived by taxicab. Sweet opened the front door and heard the yelling of the mob.

Ossian Sweet House, Detroit, Michigan.

"Niggers! Niggers! Get the damn niggers!" Sweet later described his feelings at that tense moment. "The whole thing, the whole situation filled me with an appalling fear—a fear that no one could comprehend but a Negro, a Negro who knew the history behind his people."[78]

With the arrival of the two newcomers there were now eleven people in the house. The residents pulled down the window shades. The crowd began throwing rocks at the house. One of the rocks broke an upstairs window. Several shots were fired from the window. Another from the porch of the house. One shot hit a White man, Leon Briener, who was standing on the back porch. "Boys, they've got me," Briener said. Those were his last words.

All eleven occupants of the house were indicted for conspiracy to commit murder.

Leaders of the Detroit chapter of the National Association for the Advancement of Colored People traveled to New York to recruit Clarence Darrow for the defense. This nationally famous attorney, who just two weeks earlier lost in the trial of *The State of Tennessee vs. Scopes* (the so-called "Scopes Monkey Trial") to the prosecutor William Jennings Brian, brought national attention to trials for the murder of Leon Briener. In the first trial, all eleven defendants were tried together. It ended in a mistrial. In the second trial Ossan Sweet's younger brother Henry, who admitted to firing from the front window, was tried alone and acquitted by an all-White jury. After Henry's acquittal, the charges against the others were dropped. The trials became known as the "Sweets Trials."[79]

The economic downturn during the 1930s brought Detroit's housing boom to a sudden end. The depression hit the mortgage industry hard. Nationally the default rate on home loans rose to as many as 1,000 every day. Nearly half of the people with mortgages were behind in their payments. [80] To address this problem, President Roosevelt signed the Homeowners Loan Act of 1933 as part of his "new deal" legislation. This act established the Home Owners' Loan Corporation (HOLC), which was authorized to purchase distressed loans with government backed bonds and then reissue amortized loans at lower interest rates (5%) to be paid over a longer period of time (15 years, later extended to 25 years).

Of course, the granting of these loans carried risk. The HOLC relied on local real estate agents with their segregationist ethics to assist them in calculating the risks. Eventually the HOLC, in consultation with local city officials, lenders, appraisers, and the real brokers, developed what were called "Residential Security" maps for 239 major American cities, including Detroit. Neighborhoods were graded on such things as the age and condition of the housing, transportation access, the proximity to amenities such as parks, and the distance from polluting industries. The economic class and employment status of residents were considered and, of course, a neighborhood's ethnic and racial composition. The grades were displayed on color coded maps: the "Best" areas were shown in green, "Still Desirable" neighborhoods were colored blue, "Definitely Declining" neighborhoods were given the color yellow, and "Hazardous" neighborhoods had a red line drawn around them. This was the beginning of the practice that became known as "redlining." Any area with just a small settlement of African Americans was automatically given the classification of hazardous. Properties in the redlined neighborhoods were not given HOLC loans.[81] The result of these policies was that African Americans were automatically ineligible for the Homeowners Loan Act.

One year after the establishment of the HOLC President Roosevelt signed another bill, the National Housing Act of 1934. This act called for the creation of a Federal Housing Administration (FHA) to insure bank mortgages. The FHA covered 80 percent of the purchase price of a home and required a fully amortized 20-year payment schedule. Drawing on the work of the HOLC, the FHA developed its own appraisal standards for backing loans. These were codified in the FHA *Underwriting Manual* in 1935. The *Manual* stipulated that:

If a neighborhood is to retain stability it is necessary that properties shall continue to be occupied by the same social and racial classes. A change in social or racial occupancy generally leads to instability and a reduction in values.[82]

The *Manual* clearly preferred suburban properties to dwellings in older, urban neighborhoods: "Older properties," it said, "have a tendency to accelerate the rate of transition to lower class occupancy."[83] Highways and expressways were seen as natural barriers to segregate neighborhoods by race and social class. "[N]atural or artificially established barriers will prove effective in protecting a neighborhood and the locations within it from adverse influences, . . . include[ing] prevention of the infiltration of . . . lower class occupancy, and inharmonious racial groups."[84]

When Black GIs returned from serving in World War II and applied for home loans guaranteed by the newly established VA, they discovered that the VA followed the guidelines of FHA. The *Underwriting Manual* and its restrictive covenants limited the homes the Black Veterans were allowed to purchase, but these homes were ineligible for a VA loan. African Americans were once again automatically ineligible for government backed financing. Twenty to thirty years later, White World War II Veterans had acquired the financial asset of a fully paid off home. Black Veterans were denied that opportunity.

After World War II, the Black residents of Detroit faced a new challenge: expressways. The overcrowded Black neighborhoods of Black Bottom and Paradise Valley, just outside the downtown area, were becoming an intolerable eyesore to suburban commuters. The need for additional capacity to handle the volumes of workers making the twice daily journey from the more distant neighborhoods of the city and the suburbs could no longer be overlooked. Mayor Jefferies came up with a plan to solve both these problems, summarized in a document entitled "The Detroit Expressway and Transit System" which he presented to the Detroit Transportation Board in February 1945. The plan called for the development of a regional transportation system that included not only freeways but also rail and bus lines. The rail system never materialized in a city so dependent on automobile production, but Jeffries' plans for expressways were adopted and can be seen in today's Detroit expressway system. The Chrysler Freeway extension, which connects I-94 and downtown, was built on land that was once Black Bottom and Paradise Valley.

Jefferies' plan was adopted in 1945, but it took fourteen years before construction began on the Chrysler Freeway. This only made conditions worse for the residents of Black Bottom and Paradise Valley. The property owners found themselves trapped. They couldn't sell property that would soon be condemned, but they needed the money from the sale to be able to move. There was little incentive to make improvements, so the "blighted areas" deteriorated further. Many of the buildings were simply abandoned by their owners.[85]

In 1949 Alfred B. Cobo was elected as Jefferies' successor. A year before Cobo's election the Supreme Court of the United States once again rendered a decision against segregation. In the case of *Shelley v. Kraemer* restrictive covenants and deeds were ruled a violation of the Fourteenth Amendment and therefore were unenforceable in the courts. Cobo ran on a platform of continued support for restrictive covenants and deeds. He was elected with 60% of the vote in what was still an overwhelmingly White city. Once installed, Cobo advocated for the elimination of Detroit's "blighted areas." His vision was to replace them with middle-class, high-rise housing as well as the expressways. The

Black community understood what Cobo's vision meant for them. The common saying among the residents of the blighted areas was that "slum removal equals Negro removal."[86]

Detroit's Black Bottom neighborhood, courtesy Henry Ford College.

Where would these displaced Negroes go? Housing officials offered little assistance. Detroit Housing Commission Secretary Harry Durban wrote a letter to families being evicted, sending the confusing message of offering them assistance while encouraging them to "make every possible effort to find housing in the local market."[87] His words in a Common Council hearing showed little compassion for those being displaced. "We can't clear slums without hardship," he said.[88]

A neighborhood being vacated by Jewish residents provided the answer. This was the second time in the city's history that African Americans moved into homes being vacated by Jewish residents. In the

1920s Jewish residents, who faced the same restricted deeds and covenants as the Blacks, migrated from "Jewtown" on Hastings Street and Black Bottom to 12<sup>th</sup> Street and Virginia Park. Now they were relocating to the northern suburbs of Southfield and Birmingham, opening the homes of Virginia Park to the African Americans being dislocated by the expressways. By the mid-1960s the formerly integrated Virginia Park neighborhood was an almost exclusively Black neighborhood. This was the neighborhood the members of The Fort chose to begin an outreach ministry to their American neighbors.

*How deserted lies the city, once so full of people!*
*How like a widow is she, who once was great among the nations!*
*She who was queen among the provinces has now become a slave."*

-Lamentations 1:1

*"The Spirit of the Lord is on me, because he has anointed me to*
*proclaim good news to the poor."*

-Jesus of Nazareth[89]

# Chapter 4

# The Challenge of Virginia Park

From the very beginning, the members of The Fort were deeply concerned about the spiritual condition of their English-speaking neighbors in the Motor City. In 1920, the congregation began holding *Sondagskool,* or Sunday School classes in the Gratiot-Six Mile area. These classes were not like American Sunday School classes. They were never intended for children from the congregation. The children of the congregation were referred to as Covenant Children. Covenant Children came from Christian homes and had been baptized. Their parents could be relied on to teach the children the stories of the Bible. The church's responsibility to Covenant Children was to teach them the Catechism.[90] It was the non-covenant children from the community, children who did not have the opportunity to learn the Bible's message from their parents, who were invited to *Sondagskool,* as they had been in the Netherlands. In addition to running the *Sondagskool,* members of the congregation started spending two evenings a week in mission work. Once again, it was the young people that took the lead in these efforts.

One of these young people was Dirk Eppinga's son, Jacob. In a 2002 interview with writer James Evanhuis, Jacob described life in the growing church. Not only was involvement with church a daily part of the young man's life, but evangelistic outreach to the people of Detroit was also a major part of his church activities.

On Monday evenings we had band rehearsal. On Tuesdays we did missionary work among the Jews. On Wednesday we attended catechism class. On Thursday nights we went to Hastings Street and did street corner mission work in the Black community. On Fridays we could stay home, but on Saturdays we had our weekly church picnic. Then, on Sundays we went as young people, every Sunday afternoon after the Dutch service, to the Marine Hospital at the foot of Alter Road and we conducted mission meetings there.

Not every young person in the church participated as enthusiastically as Jacob Eppinga. Lewis Smedes also recorded his experiences as a young man in the church in his memoir.[91] Smedes found the long, stoic services at The Fort boring. "I invented techniques for tucking my chin between my fingers so that I could sleep through the sermon without my head bobbing for everybody to see," he writes. While services at The Fort bored him, Smedes found other much more exciting opportunities that captured his interests. One of those he called the "flesh pots" downtown, a reference to the sinful "flesh pots of Egypt" to which the redeemed Israelites of the Old Testament wanted to return during their long wanderings in the wilderness.[92] On Saturday afternoons Smedes would take the streetcar downtown where he would do some shopping and buy a hamburger and a beer at one of the "scruffy cafés." Once it got dark, Smedes "would walk over to the Uptown Burlesque and settle into a balcony seat to take in a forbidden show. Stars like Rose La Rose and Ruby La Rue brought my testosterone to a wicked boil." The guilt and shame young Smedes felt for attending such shows when even attendance in the regular theater was forbidden was unbearable. "How could a Christian young man of eighteen expect to get right with God while . . . he was awakening unthinkable lusts by watching wicked women take their clothes off on Saturday evenings?" To make matters worse, Smedes discovered a preference for revival meetings. "Big-time show evangelists like Bob Jones and Gypsy Smith seemed to speak more directly to my soul than did the sedate preacher at Aunt Jessie's church."

By the time the congregation purchased the property on Maryland Street, several *Sondagskool* classes composed primarily of Roman Catholics as well as a class for Negroes were being held.[93] That effort was left behind with the old building when the congregation moved into their new facility. But the work at the Marine Hospital continued. Two future Christian Reformed ministers, Reverend Jacob Eppinga and Reverend Duane VanderBrug participated in this effort, and the evangelistic meetings gave them as well as oth ers like the Hoekstra brothers—Tom, John, Henry, and Albert—opportunities for developing their emerging preaching skills. Fifty years after Jacob's father Dirk stood and made his Profession of Faith in Dutch, the congregation accepted a new challenge. According to their Fiftieth Anniversary Book, published in 1964,

> We were, and are, a highly favored people. We have been told: "let your light so shine before men, that they may see your good works and glorify your Father in heaven." This is a great task and a most important one! We have been active in establishing mission projects with a view to spreading the light of the gospel in areas where it is not sought or cared for.[94]

One of those areas where the gospel "is sought or cared for" in the eyes of these anniversary celebrants was the Virginia Park neighborhood, the former Jewish community where African Americans displaced by expressways were moving and the site of the start of the July, 1967 rebellion. A proposal was made to the congregation on their 50th Anniversary Year to establish a mission work among the residents of Virginia Park. The congregation enthusiastically embraced this new opportunity.

There is something sweet and innocent in the church members naiveté. "We have been active in establishing mission projects with a view to spreading the light of the gospel in areas where it is not sought or cared for," they said. These were Dirk Eppinga's spiritual heirs. They knew who they were. "We were, and are, a highly favored people," they said. They were *Afgescheidenen,* "Separatists." *Christian* (italics mine) Reformed. Men and women who were deeply aware of the spiritual dangers of "Worldly Amusements." They knew their identity, and they knew their mission. "We have been told: 'let your light so shine before men, that they may see your good works and glorify your Father in heaven.'"

What they most likely didn't know, or at least fully understand, was their dark, spiritual opponent, Jim Crow. "We have been active in establishing mission projects with a view to spreading the light of the gospel in areas where it is not sought or cared for," they said. They most likely did not fully understand the demonic powers of violence, Real Estate "ethics," restrictive covenants and deeds, forced dislocation, and discriminatory government practices that they were up against. These evil forces formed Virginia Park. President Johnson's 1967 National Advisory Commission on Civil Disorders, the so-called "Kerner Report," published following the 1967 disturbance that began in the community, documented the physical condition of the neighborhood:

On either side of 12th Street were neat, middle class districts. Along 12th Street itself, however, crowded apartment houses created a density of more than 21,000 per square mile, almost double the city average. The movement of people when the slums of Black Bottom had been cleared for urban renewal had changed 12th Street from an integrated community to an almost entirely Black one, in which only a number of merchants remained White. Only 18 percent of the residents were homeowners. Twenty-five percent of the housing

84

was considered so substandard as to require clearance. Another 19 percent had major deficiencies.[95]

But the spiritual condition of the community was more difficult to assess. The people of The Fort most likely did not fully understand that "spreading the light of the gospel in areas where it is not sought or cared for" would eventually force them to deal with the American demon of racism.

Nor did the people of The Fort understand that Virginia Park was not devoid of light. For example, one of the children who began attending the church and lived in the Virginia Park neighborhood was named Jarrett Bell. For Jarrett, it was home. It was a neighborhood with both beauty and issues, like any other community. In the winter after a snowfall Jarrett would shovel people's driveways and walkways. For him it was a big hustle, a way to make some quick money. But there was one neighbor whose snow Jarrett shoveled for free. She was a woman in her 60's, and her husband was a barber. In the summertime she had the most beautiful flowerbed on the block, which she regularly tended wearing a sundress. Jarrett always shoveled the woman's walks for free out of his deep respect for her. The woman's name was Rosa Parks."[96]

The residents of Grosse Pointe lived in their own kind of darkness, a spiritual darkness that also needed "the light of the gospel." The darkness of Grosse Pointe would be exposed over the next several years as the same Jim Crow attitudes and behaviors at work on the Detroit side of the border could also be found in the Pointes. The residents of Grosse Pointe may have lived in material luxury, but many of them suffered from spiritual poverty. Human thriving requires a soft heart for those who are less fortunate, whether their misfortune comes from racial prejudice, poverty, sickness, trauma, bad choices, or any combination of these and numerous other struggles that result in human suffering.

What the members of The Fort did not fully understand at the time was that their gospel message was insufficient to address the darkness of a place like Virginia Park. They believed that they ". . . have in this activity a unique work in the extension of the Kingdom of Christ for which we should be thankful and should pray that through this work many will be brought to know Christ as their Savior."[97] Their Gospel (the word means "good news") was a spiritual message that required a change of individual hearts, the seeking of personal salvation and a guarantee of a place in Heaven after death. These are certainly valid concerns. Exposing the sin found in individual hearts and the call to repentance and forgiveness are at the very heart of the Christian message. The offer of salvation is certainly a message of hope and inspiration. Offering guidance for people facing the final battle of death and providing answers for what follows is the task of every faith. But this Gospel message was incomplete. It did not address the very real suffering caused by years of racism, exploitation, poverty, and lack of access to government programs like VA loans. Their spiritual message remained silent on these very real social problems. They did not yet understand the wisdom of men like Forrester B. Washington, who said, "You cannot do much for a man spiritually until you have given him a healthy and wholesome physical environment. In other words, 'you cannot grow lilies in ash barrels.'" Dr. King had not yet given his speech at Grosse Pointe High School, a speech in which he articulates the spiritual message of Evangelical Christianity with a power that can only come from a Baptist preacher:

I believe in changing the heart. I happen to be a Baptist preacher and that puts me in the heart-changing business and Sunday after

Sunday I'm preaching about conversion and the need for the new birth and regeneration. I believe that there's something wrong with human nature. I believe in original sin not in terms of the historical event but as the mythological category to explain the universality of evil, so I'm honest enough to see the gone-wrongness of human nature so naturally I'm not against changing the heart.[98]

The members of The Fort would undoubtedly have agreed with Dr. King at this point. But the Civil Rights leader would continue. "I do feel that that is the half-truth involved here." Until hearts are changed, King would argue, laws must be passed to restrain human evil.

It may be true that morality cannot be legislated, but behavior can be regulated. It may be true that the law cannot change the heart but it can restrain the heartless. It may be true that the law can't make a man love me, but it can restrain him from lynching me, and I think that's pretty important also.[99]

Both Washington and King were saying that the darkness of places like Virginia Park was not just spiritual, but social as well. The personal, inward darkness found in human hearts must indeed be addressed, but so must the societal darkness that produces such evils as poverty, racism, Jim Crow, and housing discrimination. The church's message of repentance from sin is as much a social message as it is a personal message. To quote Jesus of Nazareth, "The Spirit of the Lord is on me, because he has anointed me to proclaim good news to the poor." He goes on and describes what this "good news" (Gospel) is: "He has sent me to proclaim freedom for the prisoners and recovery of sight for the blind, to set the oppressed free, to proclaim the year of the Lord's favor."[100]

Jesus makes no mention of Heaven or of changing human hearts. People will never thrive if their spiritual needs are met while their social needs are ignored.

Reverend Harold Botts talking with some of the youth at Community Christian Reformed Church. (Courtesy of the Botts family)

Reverend Harold Botts spearheaded this effort, and no one was better equipped for the task. A tall, athletic man full of energy, he was impatient with the pastoral style common in the day. Pastors of churches like The Fort spent most of their day in the office, waiting for the people to come to them. Reverend Botts brought the church to the people. Mornings were spent in the office doing administrative work and preparing services for the following Sunday, but once noon hit it was out onto the streets and visiting people in their homes. Walking the streets gave Reverend Botts opportunities to meet children who attended Sunday School classes and teenagers who came to Youth Group. The job of a pastor, in Bott's mind, was to bring the Good News (Gospel) to the community, and then become an advocate for the community. And the Virginia Park community needed an advocate.[101]

With the support of both The Fort and the Dearborn CRC, Reverend Harold Botts conducted a study of the area. Reverend Botts leased space on the first floor of an apartment building located on the corner of 14th Street and Pingree, where he began services almost immediately. Much of the first floor of the building was actually below ground level and so was referred to as the "basement." With the support of the denomination's Board of Home Missions he eventually purchased the entire building and began renovating the second floor to provide a more spacious place for conducting worship services as well as Sunday School classrooms.

The members of The Fort had high hopes for this new work. "We have in this activity a unique work in the extension of the Kingdom of Christ for which we should be thankful and should pray that through this work

Photo courtesy of the Botts Family

many will be brought to know Christ as their Savior," they said.[102] Two carpenters from the church, brothers John and Martin Batts, donated their time and skills to turn the basement into a functional facility for the worship and educational needs of a church. The name chosen for this new church was the Community Christian Reformed Church.

The work was successful. African Americans in Virginia Park embraced the teachings of The Fort, if not its traditions. And as we will see, this created new challenges for the members of the mother church.

When Reverend Botts first met with members of The Fort to present his plan to interested mem-bers of the congregation, two couples were sitting in the front row: Melvin and Barbra VanderBrug and Dave and Eloise Cooke. The VanderBrugs and Cookes agreed to attend the new congregation every Sunday, while keeping their membership papers at The Fort. Melvin VanderBrug's brother, Duane, was at the time co-pastor with Reverend Gordon Negen of the Manhattan Christian Reformed Church in the Harlem neighborhood of New York City. The Harlem church was the first effort by the Christian Reformed Church to establish a ministry in an African American community. Melvin's interest in Reverend Botts' proposed effort in Detroit was influenced by his brother's work and his parents' progressive views. David Cooke was a member of the denominational Home Missions Board representing the region that included Detroit. David was never completely comfortable at The Fort. When he asked to make Profession of Faith and join the church, he was required, like all young people, to meet with the elders of the church. One of the questions he was asked was whether or not he ever attended the theater. Cooke truthfully acknowledged that he did. Things had changed since the days of Dirk Eppinga. Cooke knew that at least one if not more of the elders at the table also attended movies from time to time. But, based on his admission that he had participated in one of the "worldly amusements," Cooke was denied church membership.[103]

Once David and Eloise Cooke made the commitment to weekly attendance at the Community Church, they decided they needed to talk about it with their children. One evening they gathered around the kitchen table with their children, seven-year-old Dave Jr. (who went by the name "Dave" to distinguish himself from his Dad) and his siblings Judy and Tom, and told them they would be going to a different church. Their new church would be much different than The Fort. Instead of the massive Reformed Cathedral, they would be worshipping in a basement. Instead of the beautiful pipe organ, singing would be accompanied by the piano.

"What's the big deal?" thought Dave. "Why are they making this such an important conversation?" For Dave, church was a necessary evil. He would later write, "I didn't care for church. It was boring, dull, compulsory. I felt like I was always getting judged, criticized, or punished for something I did at church."[104] For Dave, going to a different church was a welcome opportunity to get away from the one he didn't care for anyway. It was more of an adventure than a spiritual mission. David and Eloise made a point of formally asking their children if the move would be all right with them. Dave thought, "Okay, why not?" His verbal answer: "Sure."

But the basement church had no more appeal to young Dave than The Fort. "You can only make a basement church so nice," he later said, "and the volunteers did their best."[105] Once the first floor was completed, with its acoustical tile ceiling, the worship space became more appealing for the young White boy from Grosse Pointe.

The building was not the only change Dave noticed. The people dressed differently. In The Fort, the men wore business suits or dress slacks with a sport coat in a subdued color like black, grey, blue, or possibly brown. Women wore dresses or a skirt and blouse, again in conservative colors and smartly tailored. In the new church, Sunday was a fashion parade. Men wore Sharkskin or more colorful suits with pointed toe shoes, often patent leather. The women usually dressed up in bright colors and wore hats. The highlight of the year was Easter, which could only be described as pageant, where the colors and hats were on full, celebratory display. Young Dave was being exposed to a different culture, learning that differences in the church were acceptable and that people with significant differences could get along together and worship together.

Dave was completely oblivious to the color of his friends' skin. He joined the Cadet Boy's Club, which began meeting on Saturday mornings. Following the club activities, Dave would spend the rest of the day and Saturday night at the home of one of his Black friends near the Community Church. One of the homes he would visit was the Horn's where his friends Michael and Maurice lived. The Horn's Virginia Park house differed from Dave's Grosse Pointe home in many ways. It wasn't as nice. Not that it exuded poverty. It's just that the furnishings were not as new, as abundant, or as neat as they were at Dave's house. Instead of being filled with stuff, it was filled with people. Lots of people. Barbara Horn, the matriarch of the house, had ten children. Her sister, Kathy Stevens, had her own brood. The Barnes' house was always crowded with family and friends. The place was filled with activity, most of the time revolving around singing and dancing. In Dave's Dutch Reformed culture, dancing was forbidden for fear that it would lead to sexual arousal. In the Horn's house, dancing was an art form, full of beauty and grace. The dancing was accompanied by singing. Detroit music: Motown. Aretha Franklin. Diana Ross and the Supremes. The Temptations. On one occasion Dave was invited to a birthday party filled with music and dancing. When he tried to join in with the fun, it made him feel awkward. It wasn't that Dave was at stereotypical White boy with no rhythm; Dave was a Dutch White boy who simply didn't know how to dance. His friends at Community Church had gifts and skills that he lacked.

Dave felt safe in the Virginia Park neighborhood. He and his friend Maurice would hang out together, wander around the neighborhood, and at times as late as 11 p.m., would head over to the neighborhood supermarket several blocks away to purchase something. But when friends from Community Church visited Dave's home in Grosse Pointe, they did not always feel welcome. For example, another of Dave's friends, Lamar Germany, would come out to Grosse Pointe on Sundays and the two would ride their bikes together. To Dave, Lamar was just another kid, but the other kids in Grosse Pointe saw things differently. One Sunday afternoon, on a local playground, one of the kids referred to Dave's friend as "Nigger." Before long, his friend was gone. He went back to the Cooke's house because he didn't feel safe.

On another Sunday afternoon Lamar and Dave were riding their bikes down the streets of Grosse Pointe Park when they were stopped by two Police Officers. Dave knew both the men. One of the officers was Officer Blair, whose beat included regular visits to Dave's school. The second was the Chief of Police, who lived next door to his aunt and uncle, Sy and Mariam Schaafsma. Dave was likely surprised, but not alarmed by being stopped by the two policemen. The patrolmen asked where the boys got the bicycles. Had they been stolen? Bicycles were often stolen in Grosse Pointe, and properly locking a bike up when not in use in such a way as to not have it stolen was both a discipline and something of a science. The two cops asked a few more questions, then let the two boys go. The incident made an impression on both boys. "Why," thought Dave, "had they stopped us?" Lamar knew the answer to Dave's unspoken question. He was clearly not welcome in Grosse Pointe.

Within the walls of the Community Church, Black and White members of the congregation coexisted peacefully, learning and growing together. As Melvin VanderBrug later said, "Exposure to this new culture changed our lives."[106] But outside the walls of the church, tensions were high. Three months after the young congregation's first birthday, a young seminary student and his wife, Richard and Barbara Grevengoed, joined Reverend Botts for a year-long internship at the church. The Grevengoeds, who were both White, moved into one of the apartments on the third floor of the building with a sunroom overlooking the corner of 14th and Pingree. The only other resident living in the fourteen-apartment building was the custodian, an African American who occupied a small apartment near the boiler room. The first floor of the building had already been gutted and turned into a worship center. The second floor was being renovated to provide much needed classroom space. Richard and Barbara, who were newlyweds, seldom saw the custodian and for the most part had the entire massive building to themselves. There were very few other White people in the community, and they were the only White members of the congregation residing in the church's neighborhood. The nation was at war in Vietnam. Blacks were being killed at much higher rates than Whites,[107] adding fuel to the fire of the community's already unaddressed anger over poor housing, inadequate education, lack of employment, and the brutality they suffered at the hands of a 90 percent White police force. Soon after Richard arrived in Detroit, he and Reverend Botts conducted the first funeral in the church's history. The deceased was a Black soldier killed in the war.

One Sunday evening during the summer while the Grevengoeds were relaxing in their apartment they noticed some commotion on the street below them. Traffic had been detoured and some sort of platform was being set up. Soon a loudspeaker system began blaring. H. Rapp Brown was holding a Black Power rally right next to the church. Right below the Grevengoeds' window. Malcolm X had been assassinated the previous year and Brown was the new leader of the radical wing of the Civil Rights movement and the voice of Black rage. The shouting began:

"Black Power!"

Years of pent-up anger at Jim Crow, at laws denying people housing based on their skin color, at being dislocated to make room for an expressway serving White suburbanites, at poor education, at the lack of job opportunities to provide for their families within a reasonable distance from their neighborhoods and especially at being occupied by a White police force whose chief means of law enforcement was brutality— a vocal river of anger raged down Fourteenth Street that Sunday afternoon.

"Black Power!"

Students from Northern High School yelling, motivated by the words of Henry David Thoreau they had read in class: *Let your life be a counterfriction to stop the machine.*

"Black Power!"

*What I have to do is to see . . . that I do not lend myself to the wrong which I condemn.*

"Black Power!"

Raised fists attacking the air.

"Black Power!"

Brown's rhetoric stoking the anger of the protesters: "If America doesn't come around, we're gonna burn it down!"

"Black Power!

"Black Power!"

"Black Power!"

For the White seminary student and his bride watching all this from their box seat view, the experience was unsettling. For the first time they really began to understand—more than understand—to *experience* themselves the rage, the deep hurt and the pain of their neighbors who were daily being exploited and demeaned. They began to understand the depth of the despair their Black brothers and sisters experienced as they were continually marginalized and degraded. They didn't judge the radical speaker. They *heard* his message. They *heard* the voices of the angry protesters. They heard the voices of men and women of color, second-class citizens who were so often the victims of racial prejudice. They heard the voices of people who had too often been tuned out and ignored since their arrival in America in the dark bowels of slave ships.

The rally was a life-changing event in their journey as Christians. They had come to Detroit to speak, to offer a message that began with judgment and ended with good news about salvation and the assurance of the afterlife. In that final summer before they returned to seminary, for the first time Richard and Barbara Grevengoed were able to *hear* the voices of those who were suffering, the cries that had so often fallen on deaf ears.

Whatever idealism Dave Cooke Jr. developed as the result of his experience at the Community Church was challenged when he was in sixth grade, a year and a half after the rebellion. He had received a guitar for Christmas. Gerry Plakmeyer, the piano player at the church and a music teacher, learned of this and brought a book on how to play the guitar to the evening service, wanting to give it to Dave. Following the service, her husband Wayne and Dave walked across 14th Street in the December darkness to get the book. Two African American men came out of nowhere. One stuck a gun in Wayne's back.

"Get in the car—we're going for a ride."

Wayne spun around and pushed the music book into the gunman's chest in defense. The stranger stepped back. He fired a shot at Wayne. The White man doubled over, a bullet in his right lung. The strangers fled.

Dave ran back into the church building. "Mr. Plakmeyer's been shot," he yelled.

Somehow Wayne Plakmeyer managed to walk up the church stairs where he was greeted by the shocked members of the congregation. They took him into the church office, made him comfortable, and called the ambulance. He was taken to Ford Hospital and treated. He survived the experience, but they never removed the nickel-plated bullet from his lung.

For years after that experience, Dave Cooke experienced a reoccurring dream of someone coming out of the darkness and shooting him. After being shot, his glasses would fall off his face. Today dreams like that would be identified as a symptom of Post-Traumatic Stress Disorder (PTSD).

The White people of Community Church, like the Grevengoeds, Wayne Plakmeyer and the Cooke family were among the first to leave the safety of churches like The Fort. As pioneers, they paid a big price for their courage in venturing outside the safety of their familiar ethnic and traditional world to live out their Christian life. Their experiences made a big impact on the Grosse Pointe congregation. Eventually the doors of The Fort would be open not just to let members out to do mission work in the city, but to allow people of all backgrounds to come in. But that would only begin to happen in the 1960s, beginning with allowing children from the Community Church to attend the Christian School run by the members of The Fort.

William Dirksen replaced the Grevengoeds as the summer intern in September 1966. He and Reverend Botts immediately made plans to host a mission team during the summer of 1967 under a denominational program called SWIM: Summer Workshop In Ministries. Botts and Grevengoed had already hosted such a team during the summer of 1966. The program recruited High School volunteers who would be expected to canvass the neighborhood around the church and enroll children for Bible School, teach classes during Bible School week, and engage in follow-up calls on the families of the children who attended. The first year the church ran the program it was a huge success. The church building was overflowing with children every morning during Bible School week. For the second year six High School volunteers, all White, were recruited from Unity Christian High School in Hudsonville, Michigan (just west of Grand Rapids): Bill VanderVliet, Tom Hopkins, Marcia Brower and Mary Schrotenboer from Hudsonville and Janice Baker and Doreen Gulker from Allendale. Bill and Tom were originally assigned to a site in Florida, but at the last minute were reassigned to Detroit. Bill was especially disappointed at the change to Detroit. Adventurous by nature, he had never been to Florida and was excited to go somewhere new. For Bill, Detroit was far less exciting. But he and Tom were good friends, and he really did want to make a difference with his life, so off they went to Detroit with the four girls, to an adventure filled with more excitement than Bill could ever imagine.

The team arrived in Detroit in early July, settled into their quarters on the top floor of the apartment building that housed the church, and went to work. All went well until the morning of Sunday, July 23, when the six youths woke up and learned that there was "a disturbance" in the neighborhood. The "disturbance" was the result of the Detroit Police Department's raid of a blind pig on 12th Street, six blocks away. Morning worship had been cancelled. Soon Reverend Botts arrived from his home in Dearborn. Long distance phone calls were immediately made to parents, reassuring them that their children were safe. Local phone calls were then made to supporters in Dearborn and Grosse Pointe to make plans for the evacuation of the six White High School kids from the burning, riot-torn neighborhood. One of the Community Church members who lived in Dearborn, Wes Benzelaar, braved the trip with his wife Helen in their yellow Chevrolet. They took the two boys and

S.W.I.M. Team members gathered in front of Hillcrest Christian Reformed Church, Hudsonville MI before beginning their service in Detroit. From left to right: Mary Schrotenboer, Doreen Gulker, Marcia Brower, Janice Baker, Tom Hopkins and Bill VanderVliet. (Courtesy Bill Vander Vliet)

headed for Dearborn, driving straight through a group of looters throwing rocks at a supermarket. That left the four girls. After numerous telephone calls between supporters in Grosse Pointe, Dearborn, and the Community Church a plan was developed. A member of the Dearborn CRC, Sam Van Til, was an executive for the A&P grocery store. He was able to get a bread truck from the supermarket chain and drove it to the Community Church to rescue the girls. They were told once the truck arrived to run like crazy to the truck, get in, and hide in the back. After passing through several police lines, they arrived safely in Dearborn where they were welcomed and cared for by members of the Dearborn church.

Meanwhile, the rebellion continued around the church. At one point, David Cooke, Sr. made a trip to the area. He discovered a number of African American residents of the apartment building across the street from the church lying down on the sidewalk, where they were being searched by National Guardsmen. Twenty to twenty-five people were standing around, watching the scene. A tank was parked in front of the church. Cooke thought about taking some photos but changed his mind when he saw a number of Detroit Police cars with black electrical tape covering any identifying numbers, their license plates folded in half making any identification impossible. One of the National Guardsmen told him to leave.

Most of the businesses targeted by the rioters were owned by Whites. To identify the Black-owned businesses, community activists would write the words "Soul Brother" on the building. Someone wrote the words "Soul Brother" on the side of the Community Church building. Reverend Botts, a White pastor, was a "Soul Brother." He had spent many hours over the last three years walking the streets of the neighborhood and offering care for the people of the community. His efforts paid off. The people of Virginia Park saw Reverend Botts as a "Soul Brother." He was one of them. The apartment building housing the Community Church came through the week undamaged.

After such an adventure, it would not be surprising if the high school students wanted to return to the safety of their homes in West Michigan. Their parents would most likely insist that they come home. This never happened. The students never considered quitting. They felt safe, supported by Reverend Botts and the members of the local churches. By the end of the week they were back living in the Community Church, but their mission had changed. The neighborhood was now in ruins. The stench of smoke hung in the humid July air. What had been apartment buildings near the church were now mounds of ashes. Fifty years earlier it was the young people who taught their Dutch fathers to sing the Psalms in English. Once again it was the young people who were the teachers. Six White High School students from West Michigan demonstrated that "You cannot do much for a man spiritually until you have given him a healthy and wholesome physical environment. In other words, 'you cannot grow lilies in ash barrels.'" The pressing concern for people living in the ashes of Virginia Park was meeting the physical needs of the traumatized community.

The following Sunday, July 30, Community Church was packed. The regular members of the congregation there were joined by a number of National Guardsmen from the Christian Reformed Churches on the western side of the state, deployed to Detroit for riot duty. Monday morning the young people began going door to door, checking on the residents and inviting the children to come to the church for Vacation Bible School. The program was held as planned.[108]

National Guardsmen gathered on Pingree Street in front of Community Christian Reformed Church (left, out of view), July 1967. Courtesy of Detroit Free Press.

*Grosse Pointe is representative of dozens of wealthy residential areas in the U.S. where privacy, unhurried tranquility, and unsullied property values are respected.*

-TIME Magazine[109]

*"Every person has the moral as well as the legal right to purchase or rent a house anywhere without limitations based on race, color, religion, or national origin. The churches and their members should lead the way in making sure that this right of every person is not violated in our own community either by accepted practices or community prejudices."*

-Grosse Pointe Ministers' Statement

## Chapter 5

# 743 North Rosedale Court

Gordon Write was an attorney, the son of a millionaire who made his money in real estate. A native of suburban Cleveland, Ohio, Gordon began his career directing the Cleveland University's Euclid Urban Renewal program and serving as Assistant Director of Law for the City of Cleveland. From there he moved to Washington, D.C. as a consultant to the Task Force for Equal Opportunity in Business. In 1966, at the urging of President Lynden B. Johnson, he accepted a position in Detroit as the Midwest Regional Director of the United States Commerce Department's Economic Development Administration.

Wright began looking for a home for his family in a community similar to the one they were moving from, the Cleveland suburb of Westley Heights, Ohio. He wanted a quiet, attractive community, one with good schools in which to raise his three children. A boating enthusiast, Wright was attracted to the private parks with boat slips and the yacht clubs all providing recreational access to Lake St Clair. So, Gordon and his wife Patricia started looking for a home to purchase in Grosse Pointe. They found a brand-new home, not yet completely finished, at 743 North Rosedale Court in Grosse Pointe Woods. They paid $43,000 cash for the house, and moved in on July 19, 1966, one year before the Detroit riots.

The Wrights were Black.

By 1966 Grosse Pointe had become a national symbol of racial segregation in the north. Unlike neighboring Detroit, where restrictive deeds and covenants kept unwanted groups out, Grosse Pointe had its own system to regulate who could move into the exclusive lakeside communities. The Grosse Pointe Property Owner's Association and the Grosse Pointe Realtors developed the "Point System" in the mid-1940s. When someone wanted to move into Grosse Pointe, a private investigator was hired to fill out a questionnaire determining whether the potential homeowner and family would be acceptable residents. Some of the questions were:

1. If not American born, how long have the applicants lived in this country?
2. Is their way of living typically American?
3. Are the husband's immediate associates typical?
4. Are their friends predominately typical?
5. Appearances—swarthy, slightly swarthy or not at all?
6. Accents—pronounced, medium, slight, not at all?
7. What is the husband's position as distinguished from his occupation?
8. How does this position stand in the public's estimation?
9. Dress—neat, sloppy, flashy or conservative?
10. Grammar—good, fair, or poor?[110]

The term "typically American" and the word "typical" were not defined, but everyone understood it meant White, Anglo-Saxon. The maximum score was 100. For most, a score of 50 or more allowed them to purchase a home in Grosse Pointe. People of Polish descent needed a score of 55. Greeks 65. Italians 75. Jews 85. Negroes and Orientals need not apply.[111]

The entire system was exposed to a national audience in April, 1960 when *The New York Times* and *Time Magazine* both ran articles about it.[112] According to the *Time Magazine* article, "Grosse Pointe is representative of dozens of wealthy residential areas in the U.S. where privacy, unhurried tranquility, and unsullied property values are respected." The article went on, referencing the community's reaction to the previous week's article in the *New York Times*: "Last week Grosse Pointe was in the throes of a rude, untranquil expose of its methods of maintaining tranquility." The article ended with a final jab at the community. "What makes neighboring Detroiters smile about the carefully protected Grosse Pointe exclusivity is that the area's permanent, well-established residents somehow include such noted Detroit gangsters as Matthew Rubino (20 arrests), Peter Licavoli (24) and John Priziola (17)." Detroit native and comedian Lily Tomlin (the telephone operator Ernestine on Rowan and Martin's *Laugh-In*) joked that although her mother's name was Ford, her Italian fruit-peddler father kept them from acquiring enough points to move into Grosse Pointe.

There was nothing funny about any of this to Grosse Pointe residents. Tranquility included being kept from the public eye. They were shocked and embarrassed by the exposure. Many were unaware that they had been subjected to such scrutiny when they had purchased their homes. Some became defensive. The Grosse Pointe Real Estate Association led the defense of the practice, suggesting that 95% of Grosse Pointe residents approved of the system as it effectively kept property values high. Others, already uncomfortable with the community's reputation for snobbery, felt guilt.[113] Michigan's Democratic Governor, G. Mennon Williams—himself a resident of Grosse Pointe—called the system "odious," while Michigan's Attorney General, Paul Adams, called it "morally corrupt."[114]

Paul Adams ordered the abandonment of the system within thirty days. If his order was violated, he promised the state would "impose all sanctions possible."[115] The Point System was dropped, but discrimination continued. Realtors would not make follow-up calls to

Black clients like they did to White,[116] and when potential Black renters tried to look at vacant apartments they would be met with such excuses as "it's rented already . . . it's not ready at all . . . the landlord had to check out a faulty this or that. . . [or] the apartment was not for rent."[117]

One of the responses to the exposure of the Point System was the formation of the Grosse Pointe Human Relations Council.[118] The Council began small, meeting in members' homes to hear people of both races speak to the challenges not only of open housing but of human relations issues in general. The group sought members who valued human rights more than property values. Their first public act was to sponsor a walk down Kercheval Avenue in Grosse Pointe's exclusive "Village" shopping district on Saturday, June 29, 1963 in support of open housing. This walk occurred just six days after the Detroit "Walk to Freedom" march down Woodward Avenue, at which Dr. Martin Luther King, Jr., gave the first rendition of his famous "I Have a Dream" speech later given on the steps of the Lincoln Memorial. Governor George Romney, Michigan's newly elected Republican governor and a devout Mormon, refused to participate in political activities on Sunday and so missed the Detroit "Walk to Freedom." But the following Saturday he unexpectedly appeared in Grosse Pointe and led the 600 marchers. According to the *Grosse Pointe News*,

> . . .as they walked, it became increasingly clear that Pointe residents intended to extend a friendly welcome. Interested watchers in the village looked on peacefully, breaking into spontaneous applause at many points. Flags were hung on poles along Kercheval. Many homes displayed flags as well, all along the route. A good number of Pointe spectators joined the ranks of the marchers as they progressed, and soon, the parade stretched at least three blocks. . . Along the route of the march, demonstrators stopped in front of two real estate offices for a

few brief minutes. The firms were singled out as "ringleaders" in the alleged Pointe discrimination.[119]

The demonstration was followed by a rally at Grosse Pointe High School attended by 1100-2000 people, 70% of whom were White and 30% Black.[120]

By 1964 the Grosse Pointe Human Rights Council was ready to organize, with a membership of a mere 79 individuals. That same year *Holiday* magazine published an article entitled, "Rich, Rich Grosse Pointe." The article included the stinging observation: "Grosse Pointe wants terribly to be liked. . . it is nervous more than anything else." One of the things they were most nervous about, according to the article, was Negroes.[121]

It was the churches, and especially the pastors of Grosse Pointe that led the drive for better race relations in the city. In 1966, when my family moved to Grosse Pointe Woods, there were 20 churches serving the spiritual needs of the residents of the five Grosse Pointes. Most of the Protestant pastors, including Reverend John Groenewold from The Fort, were part of The Grosse Pointe Ministerial Association. One month after our family arrived, twenty-six pastors representing all but two of the churches in Grosse Pointe, including the four Catholic parishes serving the community, signed a statement calling for open housing in Grosse Pointe. The entire statement read as follows:

### Grosse Pointe Ministers Statement

As ministers of churches in the Grosse Pointe community, we believe the time has come for a clear statement of religious conviction and democratic principle on the matter of race relations in our community and in the metropolitan area of which it is a part. We cannot separate ourselves from the currents of change and the new patterns of human relationships that are moving forward in America and throughout the world today. To attempt to do so is to betray our common democratic heritage and Judeo-Christian ethics which our churches, through their respective denominations, represent.

Therefore, we state our support of and loyalty to the following propositions:

1. Every person has the moral as well as the legal right to purchase or rent a house anywhere without limitations based on race, color, religion, or national origin.

2. The churches and their members should lead the way in making sure that this right of every person is not violated in our own community either by accepted practices or community prejudices.

3. Freedom of opportunity for all persons in housing, education, employment, use of public facilities, and enjoyment of the advantages our community offers must be supported and encouraged unequivocally now.

4. We pledge ourselves and urge our church members and fellow citizens to welcome into their neighborhoods all responsible persons of whatever race, color, religion, or national origin. We stand ready to work with our neighbors along these lines to create a more desirable community for all.

In taking this stand we emphasize the fact that it is supported and sanctioned by the teaching of the several churches and denominations to which we belong, as well as the Constitution of the United States, the Supreme Court of the United States, the Constitution of the State of Michigan, numerous laws passed by state legislatures and the Congress of the United States.

The statement has been signed by the following members of the clergy: Harold W. Abram, Bertram deHeus Atwood, Ralph V. Barton, Franklin P. Bennett, Jr., P.L. Colgan, Lawrence F. Graven, John H. Groenewold, Gary R. Gruber, Robert C. Hastings, Dale Ihrie, Paul F. Keppler, Richard S. Knight.

Also: Richard G. Kenning, George E. Kurz, Eriville B. Maynard, Harry C. Meserve, Richard W. Mitchell, Frank J. McPhillips, James D. Nixon, Andrew F. Rauth, Charles W. Sandrock, Philip M. Stahl, Ben L. Tallman, Paul A. Winchester, George R. Whitney and Edgar H. Yeoman.

The statement was read from the pulpits of a number of Grosse Pointe churches the following Sunday, including the prestigious Grosse Pointe Memorial Church (United Presbyterian). It is unknown whether the statement was read from the pulpit of The Fort, but most likely it was not as it would have upset too many people. Four months later, the Wrights moved into Grosse Pointe Woods.

It was not easy for the Wrights to purchase a home in Grosse Pointe. They originally saw a classified advertisement for a home in Grosse Pointe that interested them and so they contacted the realtor and arranged for a showing. When they met the realtor, they sensed some hesitancy on his part. Mr. Wright asked the realtor, "Is it giving you trouble to try to help me?" to which the realtor replied, "Yes, it would. I might lose my business."

"Ok," said Mr. Wright, "I'll do it another way."

Gordon Wright was not interested in moving to Grosse Pointe to break the color bar. "I'm not preoccupied with fighting these things out through legal machinery," he said. "I don't have time to be a test case." So, rather than relying on the brokers, Wright began driving up and down the streets of Grosse Pointe noting homes with "For Sale" signs. They found one they liked, a two-story colonial with red brick and white siding. Gordon Wright persuaded his friend, fellow lawyer John Fillion, to act as a "straw buyer." Homes in the area ranged in price from $35,000 to $40,000. The Wrights paid a premium price for the house.

111

But trouble was inevitable. Gordon Wright had moved into an all-White neighborhood just 10 miles from where the Black Dr. Ossan Sweet had faced a White mob protesting his moving into their all-White neighborhood 41 years earlier.

On moving day, neighbors welcomed them with a pitcher of lemonade. But that evening others drove by shouting, "Nigger, get out!" Friendly neighbors offered Patricia curtains to cover the picture window. According to the Grosse Pointe Woods police blotter that evening, a neighbor approached a police officer stationed near the Wright's home. "How are things going?" he asked.

"Fine, thanks, only it's hot," the officer answered.

"Not you, the situation down the street," the neighbor replied.

The policeman said he knew nothing about it. The neighbor said he did, and he had spoken with a lawyer who knew who bought the house and sold it to the "colored family." The neighbor went on, "This sort of thing can't happen in Grosse Pointe. You can take it for what it's worth, you boys better get prepared. You boys better get ready because there's going to be trouble." The blotter identified this neighbor as a potential instigator of trouble.

Police began keeping track of the license plates of the many cars parading past the White's house. About half the cars were registered to residents of Grosse Pointe, the other half to residents of other nearby suburbs including Harper Woods, St. Clair Shores, and Detroit. Three days after the Writes moved in, the Kiwanis Club bus heading for the lakefront pool park slowed down in front of the Wright's home. The children leaned out of the windows and yelled. The bus driver denied the incident.

The incidents continued, both positive and negative. One St. Clair Shores man went door to door to try to find the colored family because he felt sorry for them and wanted to welcome them. Another St. Clair Shores man with two teenagers threw firecrackers on the Wright's property.

Meanwhile, a group of neighbors living two blocks away from the Wright's house filed a formal complaint to the mayor of Grosse Pointe Woods and the Common Council, complaining of the cost of the extra police protection the Wrights were getting. They pointed out there had been no problem or disturbance in the area, and this was an unnecessary use of tax dollars. Others complained of the traffic the Wright's presence brought. A Detroiter asked one of the neighbors where the Wright's house was. The neighbor refused to tell the man, who promised as he was leaving that he would burn the house down. Another Detroit man, when questioned by the police as to why he was lingering near the Wright home, replied, "I'm just watching the nigger's house. What the hell are you guys watching the nigger for? Go watch some of the other guys' homes."[122]

The mayor of Grosse Pointe Woods commented that he thought everyone in the city knew of the Wright's move within 24 hours of the Wright's move. "Offhand," he continued, "I'd say that where reactions were known, the majority reaction was one of disapproval." How the residents of the city all knew of the Wright's move is something of a mystery. Nothing appeared in *The Detroit News* or *The Detroit Free Press* until more than a week after the Wright's move. The *Grosse Pointe News* made no mention of it. Even the weekly *Michigan Chronicle*, catering to the Black market, never mentioned the Wright's move, although if they had, it is doubtful may Grosse Pointers would have read it there.

*The Detroit News,* which served a primarily suburban readership, was focused that week on the violence in Brooklyn, NY; Jacksonville,

FL; and especially Cleveland, Ohio, all caused, according to the paper, by Negroes. The frontpage article on July 19, the day the Wright's moved into Grosse Pointe, ran under the headline: "Negroes Riot in Cleveland: Woman Killed, 2 Men Shot, 10 Buildings Burn." The article continued on page eight, where readers saw two other articles: "Negro Woman Shot in N.Y. Racial Clash" and "Violence Flares in Jacksonville as Negroes March on City Hall." The next night, July 20, the *News* ran a front-page article entitled: "Cleveland Gets More Troops: 2nd Negro Killed in 2nd Night of Riots, Burnings." It gave the grim statistics:

> Two killed by gunfire.
> At least 24 injured, including 12 policemen, a fireman and five persons with gunshot wounds.
> Uncounted property damage from burning and looting.
> More than 100 arrests. . .
> Ruined, blackened hulks of buildings, smashed store windows, heaps of tangled rubble—these were the ugly remains.

The article went on, giving all the gory details of what was going on in Cleveland:

> Officers armed with rifles were posted on buildings.
> A police helicopter with its lights off again clattered overhead in the night.
> The air was filled with screaming sirens.
> A firebomb, made of a bottle of gasoline, with a rag for a wick, flew from a car occupied by Negroes. Flames gushed from a bar. Fire spread to another building.
> A Negro policeman trying to clear a street of Negroes said: "I'm telling you now, if anybody shoots at me, I'm going to shoot back."

The third night, July 21, gave a closer look at the tragedy. "Cleveland Mother, 16, Shot in Riot," was the title of the front-page article. In addition to the young mother's age being part of the headline, it was repeated twice in the article, reinforcing common stereotypes of poor Black women having children at young ages to get welfare checks. The two children, ages 4 and 7 months, were also hurt in the incident, which occurred when she and her husband were driving down a street in one of the affected areas of Cleveland. Such articles certainly did nothing to calm the fears of those concerned about a Negro family moving into their neighborhood in Grosse Pointe Woods.

Three nights in a row *The Detroit News* ran front page articles on the rioting by Negroes in Cleveland, including details about a sixteen-year-old Black mother of three who was shot. But there was no mention of the White people in Grosse Pointe who were throwing firecrackers on the lawn of Gordon Wright—a Black lawyer and son of a millionaire—and shouting "Nigger, get out!"

One person who was very aware of the Wright's moving into Grosse Pointe Woods was John Feikens, a resident of Grosse Pointe Park and member of The Fort. Feikens had been appointed as a Federal Judge by President Eisenhower to fill a vacancy on the United States District Court for the Eastern District of Michigan but stepped down from that position a year later when his nomination was not confirmed by the Senate. He was later re-nominated to that position in 1970 by President Nixon, where he served until his death in 2011. In 1966 Feikens was serving as the co-chairman of the Michigan Civil Rights Commission. Two days after the Wright's move, the Commission sent a letter, or "Fact Sheet," to community leaders including the pastor of every church in Grosse Pointe. The letter was written: "TO: The Residents of Grosse Pointe Woods. RE: Recent home purchased by a Negro family." It began by observing, "The purchase of a new home by a Negro family this week in Grosse Pointe Woods has prompted considerable speculation and rumor." Point number one in the letter was labeled, "Who?" and gave a brief background of Mr. and Mrs. Wright, pointing out that "Mr. Wright accepted . . .[his] post [as the Economic Development Administration, U.S. Department of Commerce] at the urging of the President of the United States." The fact sheet went on and pointed out, "The Wrights have purchased the house with their own funds." The Wrights, according to the Fact Sheet, purchased the home from a friend who purchased it from a Real Estate Broker "because he did not believe that he would have been able to buy the house directly from the broker had it been known that he was a Negro." The Fact Sheet then addressed the important question; "Will this affect property values?" by pointing out:

> The assumption that property values deteriorate when a Negro family purchases a home in a previously all-White neighborhood is without foundation. Numerous studies conducted by economists and appraisers have demonstrated that property values remain constant or even increase under these circumstances. The only exception is a temporary depreciation if a great number of property owners in the same neighborhood panic and put their property up for sale at the same time. . . The likelihood of such an occurrence in Grosse Pointe Woods is extremely remote, if for no other reason than the market for homes in the $35,000-$40,000 price-range is highly limited.[123]

Fr. Ralph V. Barton, pastor of Our Lady Star of the Sea Catholic Church, the parish serving North Rosedale Court, read the "Fact Sheet" from his pulpit on Sunday, July 24—the first Sunday after the Wright's move. "We didn't actually preach a sermon on it," he later told a reporter, "but merely commented that this was a factual report, and that they should be guided by it rather than rumor. We advised our people to treat the whole thing calmly and to accept what had happened in a neighborly way."

Fr. Edgar Y. Yeoman, rector of St. Michael's Episcopal Church in Grosse Pointe Woods, also read the Fact Sheet that Sunday "so that people would have the true facts, rather than depending on rumors." He later commented, "I find evidence of no organized or even sizable opposition in the parish, although there were some extra-ordinary rumors around. In matters of this kind you always are surprised at how people perform. I am proud of a good many of our people and disappointed at the conduct of some others."

It is unlikely that the Fact Sheet was read from the pulpit of The Fort that Sunday morning. For one thing, the Wrights lived on the other side of Grosse Pointe from The Fort, and so did not directly affect the members. More importantly, there was a conversation going on among the members of the congregation as to whether it was appropriate for the church to be involved in such social concerns. The Unitarian Church, a congregation that did not even believe in the Holy Trinity, was leading these efforts, supported by the Liberal Episcopal and Presbyterian churches. Could members of a church as conservative as The Fort work with such churches, whose doctrine was so much different than theirs? The question was sincere and heartfelt.

Jack Nyenhuis was one member of The Fort who believed the church could and should work with Christians of other backgrounds. A professor of Greek at Wayne State University, Nyenhuis looked the part of a University Professor with his well-groomed beard and sport jacket. I recall he always brought his own Bible to church with him—the New English translation. This clearly identified him as progressive (or "liberal") in a church where the pew and pulpit Bibles were all in the

King James translation. Jack was a member of the Human Relations Council and the daughter organization the Open Housing Committee. The Open Housing Committee was started as a sub-committee of the Human Relations Council three months after the Wrights moved to Grosse Pointe Woods. Its purpose was to provide "the vehicle whereby the growing numbers of Grosse Pointers interested in positive action for open housing can work together toward this end."[124] Nyenhuis owned a home on Lakepointe Avenue which he rented to a Black bachelor, Bill Tucker, who worked at Jacobson's Department Store in the exclusive Village Shopping District. This was the first time a Black person rented a house in Grosse Point. Nyenhuis and the members of the Open Housing Committee were concerned about publicity, and intentionally sought to keep the event low-key.

One week after the Wright's move into the Grosse Pointe Woods, John Feikens, the Federal Judge from The Fort, and Circuit Judge Blair Moody Jr., the new president of the Human Relations Council, met with a group of around 100 residents at the Central Library. At that meeting, sponsored by the Grosse Pointe Human Rights Council, the two men spoke out strongly against racial prejudice. Feikens told the audience of similar incidents around the state, including Birmingham, Bloomfield Hills, and Saginaw. He assured those present that the trouble would blow over quickly, and that the presence of the Writes and other Black families would not depress property values. Judge Blair Moody identified the Human Relations Council as the "laymen's arm of the Grosse Pointe churches."

It was Harold Schacern, the Religion Writer for *The Detroit News*, who finally broke the story of the Wright's move into Grosse Pointe to the newspaper's readers. His front-page article began: "A community's moral fiber smothered its prejudices last night as Grosse Pointers at a public meeting accepted without protest the arrival of their first Negro neighbors." Schacern gave credit to the churches of Grosse Pointe for their leadership. "[The meeting] ended in tranquility and as a salute to the churches of many faiths in Grosse Pointe whose lay and clerical leaders have long prepared for just such a happening."[125] That same day *The Detroit Free Press* quoted Gordon Wright as saying that the trouble was diminishing every day, just as John Feikens predicted the previous evening. Wright said he had expected a better reception given the educational and economic level of the community. "But," he said graciously, "I'm not bitter. These are human beings with human frailties. In any given community there are a few who don't measure up."[126]

Gordon Wright might have believed that the trouble was diminishing, but it was not over. The morning after the reports came out in *The Detroit News* and *The Detroit Free Press* an unidentified caller to police headquarters in Grosse Pointe Woods said, "Trouble at Rosedale Court tonight," and threatened to run the Wrights out of town. Another woman called that same day saying she overheard that there might be a race riot in Detroit that night, and if that happened some local teenagers were planning to get together and wreck the Wright's house. Five extra patrolmen were called into work, and an extra police car was assigned to the area. Nothing happened that evening.

Two days after Gordon Wright moved into Grosse Pointe Woods, his soon to be assistant, Glenn Brown, also moved into the Pointes. He found a house in Grosse Pointe Park that he was able to rent directly from its owner. The Browns were assisted by the Grosse Pointe Human Relations Council, which encouraged them to stay at home for a few days to prevent incidents such as the Wright's had experienced. Unlike the Wrights, the Browns were welcomed into their new community and experienced no opposition to their presence. They developed a good relationship with several other couples in the neighborhood and remained friends with them even after they moved away.

They refused newspaper interviews and instead immediately got involved in the community including becoming the first minority member of the Human Rights Council.

Four months after moving to Grosse Pointe Woods, Gordon Wright's and Glenn Brown's jobs were phased out in an economy measure and the office was moved to Duluth, Minnesota. The Wright's hoped to sell their home to another Black family, but that was not to happen. Overall, Gordon Wright considered the experience a positive one, especially for the community. In an interview five years later, he pointed out that property values had actually gone up in the short time he lived in Grosse Pointe. "It is important that the community have more cultural enrichment," he said. "It should not be a sterile White community." He added that he believed the experience helped give the community greater cultural consciousness.[127]

Glenn Brown tried to find a job in Detroit but was unsuccessful. The Browns left Grosse Pointe three months after the Wrights. They spent a year in Washington D.C. with the Peace Corps and then relocated overseas. He said he would encourage anyone, Black or White, to live in Grosse Pointe and take advantage of the good schools and community services.[128]

As the Wright's were contemplating moving, they told a reporter, "We've met a lot of very wonderful people here, and we would hate to leave."

*"Nineveh has more than a hundred and twenty thousand people who cannot tell their right hand from their left, and many cattle as well. Should I not be concerned about that great city?"*

-Jonah 4:11

*"You cannot do much for a man spiritually until you have given him a healthy and wholesome physical environment. In other words, 'you cannot grow lilies in ash barrels.'"*

-Forrester B. Washington[129]

*"If social developments continue to follow the present course, life on earth will become less and less a heaven and more and more a hell. Our society is losing touch with Christ; it lies in the dust bowed down before Mammon."*

-Abraham Kuyper[130]

# Chapter 6

# Not an Easy Church to Pastor

The Fort was not an easy church in which to be a pastor. Its membership was full of diversity in a day and a religious tradition where uniformity was expected and valued.

For example, there was social diversity. In addition to John Feikens and Jack Nyenhuis, whom we met in previous chapters, her membership included Dr. Phil Feringa, who later became one of the leading heart and vascular surgeons in the country. Don Van Wingerden was co-owner of Smedeson Steel company, which distributed the large steel beams used in commercial construction. Feikens, Feringa, and Van Wingerden lived in impressive homes "below Jefferson," south of Jefferson Avenue and close to Lake St. Clair, the exclusive neighborhood of Grosse Pointe Park. Nyenhuis lived north of Jefferson in Grosse Pointe Park along with Bob Melling, who sold life insurance. On the Detroit side of Mack Avenue was the two-story working-class bungalow of Hemmo Schreuder who drove a truck for Van Wingerdan's Smedeson Steel, and two brothers named Batts who made their living in the building trade. And then there was Mabel Semmelman, a beloved member of the congregation who lived in near-poverty with her son Billy, had no Dutch blood in her at all, and had to be picked up for church twice every Sunday by one of the members of the church council.

There was social diversity in The Fort during the 1960s, but that was not what made it difficult to pastor. The real diversity that caused tension in the congregation was the diversity in thinking and perspective. At home I learned two words to help me understand this diversity. Some

123

people were called "Conservatives." My Dad was a Conservative, so I learned that Conservatives were the good guys. It was possible for a Conservative to "go off the deep end," which posed its own dangers, but this was not as bad as the threat of the Liberals to the faith. Conservatives valued the unique traditions of the Christian Reformed Church and were generally opposed to most change; especially in the way things were done on Sunday morning. The worst sin for a hardcore Conservative, at least as I understood it, was not reading the Ten Commandments in worship on Sunday morning. A true Conservative always attended the evening service and never considered not sending his (the men seemed to think for the entire family) children to the Christian School. The most Conservative of the congregational members, those in danger of going off the deep end, subscribed to and read a magazine called *The Outlook*. This magazine kept its readers informed about something called the "slippery slope" that the church was always on the verge of going down if it followed the latest liberal trends.

On the other hand were the "Liberals." I learned how to instantly spot a Liberal—they wore a beard (women didn't seem to fall into such categories). As odd as this may sound, it makes sense in the context of the 1960s. A rock group from Great Britain called the Beatles made its first appearance on the Ed Sullivan Show in 1964. In addition to their new style music, the members of the band sported long hair. This was a radical change from the short, military style haircuts popular in the 1950s and early 1960s and caused great anxiety among the conservatives. The Bible was clear on appropriate grooming standards for men. "Doth not even nature itself teach you, that, if a man have long hair, it is a shame unto him?" (I Corinthians 11:14 KJV). While my father never used Biblical passages like this so support his position, it was clear that he did not care for facial hair on men.

124

Liberals were always questioning everything. They would point out the drawbacks of the Christian School, suggesting that the children who attended were "sheltered," and might not be fully ready to face the challenges of the world when they became adults. Liberals were not as faithful in attending the evening service. As we saw in the previous chapter, they were willing to work with other churches, "liberal" churches (including the Unitarians that didn't even believe in the Trinity) when it came to social issues.

Like the rest of America, social issues were the focus of the serious conversations at The Fort during the late 1960s, and the split between Conservatives and Liberals was a microcosm of the nation as a whole. As early as 1950, social issues dominated the headlines in Detroit. In January of that year Alfred Cobo was installed as mayor of the City of Detroit, promising to uphold Detroit's restrictive racial covenants and to oppose the "Negro Invasion" of White neighborhoods.[131] On the national scene, Senator McCarthy's political rhetoric in the Senate against communism was matched by the fiery preaching of Reverend Carl McIntire from the pulpit of the Collingswood Bible Presbyterian Church, whose building was deliberately built to look like Independence Hall in Philadelphia.[132] In the Christian Reformed Church, the 1950s brought a whole new wave of post-war immigration from the Netherlands, primarily to Canada. These new immigrants were more concerned with the social ramifications of the Christian faith than on personal piety as were their fellow believers south of the border. Suddenly the uniformity of the denomination was being challenged by not only differences in thinking but also the challenge of being a bi-national denomination.[133] The pastor of The Fort during the late 1950s was Reverend Samuel Vander Jagt, "a very energetic man and a crusader against all forms of evil, which made him a tireless worker. Reverend

Vander Jagt was well read and kept in touch with all current events of the day. His quotations from religious thinkers were a challenge to memory."[134] Vander Jagt served only 3 years in Detroit before accepting a call to a church in California. I remember as a child hearing that Reverend Vander Jagt was encouraged by members of the congregation to move on. The Fort was not an easy church in which to be a pastor with the diversity of thinking and perspective among its members.

The new decade opened with the election of a young new president, John F. Kennedy who stood before Congress less than one month after the failed Bay of Pigs invasion of Cuba. After acknowledging the Soviet Union's head start in the space program, he challenged the nation to "commit itself to achieving the goal, before this decade is out, of landing a man on the moon and returning him safely to the earth."[135] Seventeen months later the Cold War with Russia came close to escalating into a full nuclear war with the Cuban Missile Crisis. Just over a year later, the young President was assassinated in Dallas, the first of three high-profile assassinations during that decade. Soon it was the War in Vietnam that was the focus of heated discussion: on the right were those fearful of the spread of Communism and on the left, those unwilling to turn a blind eye on the atrocities of war. In June 1967—one month before the Detroit rebellion—Israel fought a six-day war with Egypt, Jordan, and Syria, resulting in the Israeli occupation of a large amount of Arab lands. During the final summer of the decade the nation witnessed both the successful achievement of Kennedy's goal of putting a man on the moon in July and the nations' youth doing drugs while listening to Rock and Roll at the Woodstock Music Festival in the Catskill Mountains of New York in August. Ten months later, in May of 1970, four students lay dead on the campus of Kent State University, shot by the Ohio National Guard.

In Detroit during the 1960s Aretha Franklin's father, Reverend C.L. Franklin, was pastor of the New Bethel Baptist Church. He organized and led the "March to Freedom" down Woodward Avenue on June 23, 1963. The crowd of 125,000 people or more was the largest civil rights demonstration up to that time in the nation. Dr. Martin Luther King, Jr. spoke at that march. Parts of his speech were repeated two months later on the steps of the Lincoln Memorial and are famously known as his "I Have a Dream" speech.

Meanwhile Malcolm X in his autobiography had identified Christianity as a White Man's Religion. "The Holy Bible in the White man's hands and his interpretations of it have been the greatest single ideological weapon for enslaving millions of non-White human beings," he wrote. Malcolm X renounced Christianity and began following Elijah Muhammad's Nation of Islam, which advocated Black self-reliance and an eventual return of Blacks to Africa. Reverend Albert Cleage of Detroit's Central Congregational Church, inspired by Malcolm X, organized the Black Christian National Movement. This movement encouraged Black churches to reinterpret Jesus's teachings to better fit the experience of Black people. Theologian James Cone of Union Theological Seminary in New York City expressed similar views, going so far as to write, "Whether Whites want to hear it or not, *Christ is Black, baby,* with all the features that are so detestable to White society."[136] On Easter Sunday, 1967, Reverend Cleage unveiled a painting by the artist Glanton Dowdell depicting a Black Madonna holding a baby Jesus. The placement of the painting in the front of the church replaced a stained-glass window of the landing of George Winthrop and the Pilgrims at Massachusetts Bay on Plymouth Rock. Earlier Cleage had said to a church member, former state representative and activist Ed Vaughn, "I am sick and tired of these pilgrims landing at Plymouth Rock. I want to get something Black up there."[137]  Soon after Reverend Cleage installed the painting, he renamed the church: The Shrine of the Black Madonna.[138]

During that tumultuous decade, The Fort was served by two pastors, Reverend John Groenewold and Dr. Franklin Steen.  I have few memories of Reverent Groenewold.  Reverend Steen made a lasting long impact on my life.  They were quite different from each other but had one thing in common: both found that The Fort was not an easy congregation to pastor with the diversity of thinking and perspective among its members.

Reverend John Groenewold was the pastor on that Sunday when we first became a part of The Fort.  Two years before we arrived, The Fort celebrated its 50th Anniversary service.  In the anniversary book Reverend Groenewold is described as "gentile, kind, self-effacing, and sincere."  The anniversary book goes on: "The minister soon found a warm place in our hearts; as does the capable and hospitable lady of the manse."[139]

Groenewold was a native of Chicago, where he owned a successful coal delivery business. In mid-life he decided to sell his business and go into the ministry. After finishing the prescribed course of study at the denomination's seminary, he and his family moved to the prairies of Minnesota, where pastors were poorly paid.  After four years in Minnesota, Reverend Groenewold received an offer from The Fort to be their pastor—an offer that would include a significant salary increase which must certainly have been enticing for a father of a growing family. He was advised by friends not to go, that The Fort was a tough church.

But, after considering the offer, Reverend Groenewold sent a letter of acceptance and made plans to move within a week. Sadly, during that week he suffered a massive heart attack that prohibited him from moving to Michigan for several months.

The Fort may have been a tough congregation to serve, but it was also a very loving church, especially in times of crisis. Get well cards and other well wishes poured into the Groenewold's Minnesota parsonage, so much so that he wrote a letter of thanks to this new congregation that would soon be his church home. I suspect that early experience contributed to the Groenewolds finding a "warm place" in the hearts of the people of The Fort.

But brewing beneath the surface on that Sunday morning in February when my family first showed up was a deep dissatisfaction on the part of some in the congregation with Reverend Groenewold. On at least two occasions he blacked out in the middle of his sermon. One of his children would go up and assist their father until he regained consciousness and could finish his message. Many thought he suffered from epilepsy, but in fact it was probably related to his heart condition. Members were understandably concerned for his safety while driving, a concern he apparently did not share. But there were deeper causes for the dissatisfaction with Reverend Groenewold, and they would continue through the tenure of his successor.

Reverend Groenewold was a traditional, old-school Christian Reformed pastor. There is a Dutch word to describe such pastors: *Dominee*. A *Dominee* is a pastor that maintains a certain image, one of dignity and even distance, which was seen as worthy of such a sacred position. The *Dominee* spoke the truth of God's Word Sunday after Sunday, in all its purity and was not to be questioned. The *Dominee* stood strong as a defender of the faith and its traditions, even if his messages were often predictable, uninspiring, and even boring. Many in The Fort, especially the tradesmen with only a high school education, found comfort and security with having a *Dominee* as pastor. Others however, those who were better educated, found such an approach stifling and outdated. They were seeking direction for the huge social problems confronting society and the city and were not afraid to take on such issues. For them, *Dominee* Groenewold was too old school.

Not that Reverend Groenewold was completely insensitive to social issues. Before leaving Chicago for seminary, Reverend Groenewold struggled with having to sell an apartment building he owned at 72$^{nd}$ and Emerald. He wrestled with the question of whether or not to sell the building to Blacks but chose not to. He was not opposed to selling his property to Blacks but did not want to be the first out of concern for angering his White neighbors. Once installed in Grosse Pointe, Reverend Groenewold joined the Grosse Pointe Ministerial Association and signed the Grosse Pointe Ministers Statement calling for open housing in March 1966.

For *Dominee* Groenewold, the challenge of a congregation made up of the conservatives who were concerned with preserving the faith, educating their children and maintaining the status quo, while providing an outlet for the religious idealism of the liberals who were becoming activists proved very difficult. In early 1967 Reverend Groenewold left Detroit for Fulton, Illinois, a rural community on the banks of the Mississippi river. The Fort was the only city church the Chicago native Groenewold served. According to Groenewold, The Fort was "too difficult a church to pastor. There are too many people who think they know more than the pastor."[140] The Fort was not an easy church to pastor with the diversity of thinking and perspective among its members.

The
**First Christian Reformed Church**
**of Detroit, Michigan**

welcomes

REV. and MRS. FRANKLIN D. STEEN
and Family

**Installation Service**
SUNDAY, JULY 2, 1967
10:00 A.M.

The people of The Fort did not have to wait long for a new pastor. On a Saturday in late June Reverend Frank Steen and his family moved into the parsonage across the driveway from The Fort and the Christian School. That morning Grosse Pointe experienced a "50 year" torrential downpour. The Young People of the church were sponsoring a Strawberry Festival that afternoon in the Christian School basement, which was complicated by the fact that there were now several inches of water on the floor. "With typical aplomb, . . .the Steens waded right in with everyone else and helped with the clean-up operation."[141]  Reverend Steen was installed as pastor on July 2, 1967.[142]  Three weeks to the day after his installation Billy Scott III threw that bottle igniting the rebellion. Welcome to Detroit.

The Fort was not an easy church to pastor.

Originally from the Patterson, New Jersey area, Reverend Steen was in no way a *Dominee*. Easy going and approachable, he preferred to be called "Frank," an unbelievably informal way to refer to the pastor. His most notable features were his male-pattern baldness (which was already present when he was 18) and his New Jersey accent, which was especially noticeable when he used the word "water," an important word used frequently when either conducting or teaching about baptism. Reverend Steen had a brilliant mind. After graduating from high school at age 16, he attended Calvin College (now Calvin University) in Grand Rapids, Michigan where his freshman year he lived in the same dormitory as Duane VanderBrug, a member of The Fort. After the two of them earned their bachelor's degrees they were classmates at Calvin Seminary, on the same campus as the college. Following their Seminary graduation, VanderBrug accepted an appointment to one of the few African American congregations in the CRC, in Haarlem, New York while Steen spent a year at Westminster Seminary in Philadelphia where he studied under the professor Cornelius Van Till. Van Till, a brilliant theologian, was part of an exodus of conservative professors from Princeton Theological Seminary that resulted in the founding of the conservative Westminster Seminary in 1929. George Marsdon, who later became a renowned historian focusing on the connections between Christianity and American Culture, lived with the Steens while they were in Philadelphia. Frank Steen taught Latin to support himself while a student and knew not only the Biblical languages (Greek and Hebrew), but also Dutch, German, and later learned Spanish. He read two books a day on everything from theology to auto mechanics.

While at The Fort he was awarded a ThD from Westminster after submitting a dissertation comparing the thinking of theologian Nathan Taylor and Charles Darwin. As a result, he was now "Dr. Franklin Steen." Those of us in Junior High catechism could not resist the joke: our pastor was "Dr. Frankenstein." I don't remember if he ever heard us call him that, but I'm sure if he had he would have laughed along with us. I never got used to calling him either Frank or Doctor. To me he was always Reverend Steen.

Rev, Doctor, Frank Steen's sharp theological mind was matched by an oversized heart. According to his daughter, Stacy, "his gift was being incredibly brilliant, but he looked like a doofus. So incredibly smart he didn't have to look smart."[143] Reverend Steen valued what whomever he was talking with valued—more than valued, he was awe-struck. He could spend an afternoon with someone who had a PhD in Chemistry or someone who was homeless—it didn't matter. In either case he would come home with exciting stories of what he had learned that day. He was never bored. According to Stacy, he would "make the comfortable uncomfortable and the uncomfortable, alienated people comfortable."[144]

Perhaps no one was more alienated in the America of the late 1960s than the Vietnam War veterans. There were at least two young men from The Fort that answered the nation's call to go to Vietnam and fight communism: Jim Groenewold, son of the former pastor, and Glenn Baatjes. Jim stayed behind in Detroit for a few months after his family moved to Illinois before reporting for duty in the Army. Two years later, with no real place to return home to, he returned to Grosse Pointe and lived with another member of the congregation on Lakepointe Avenue, in a house just across the ally from the Steens. At least once a week, Reverend Steen would cross the ally, ask Jim if he had a beer, and together they would sit on the back steps of Jim's house engaging in conversation. Glen Baatjes also spent a great deal of time in the Steen home. I remember returning to The Fort years later as an ordained pastor and speaking with Glen. He bragged about the ministry of Reverend Steen. Glen experienced in the ministry of Reverend Steen the unconditional love for all that is the ideal of the Christian faith, but so seldom a reality. Reverend Steen understood deep in his soul this love for neighbor—and he practiced it, without effort. Love came naturally to him.

It was Reverend Steen's wife, Aliceanne, who upset some of the more traditional members of The Fort. While Mrs. Groenewold, found a warm place in their hearts as the capable and hospitable lady of the manse, Aliceanne could only be described as a feminist, which was not the appropriate image for a pastor's wife in the late 1960s in the conservative Christian Reformed Church. Soon after her arrival she indulged her artistic cravings by painting one of the bedrooms of the parsonage red. Fire engine red. All four walls, plus the ceiling. The "red room" remained a legend among the people of The Fort until the wife of Reverend Moxey, two pastors later, finally painted it a more suitable color.

Aliceanne then pushed the boundaries of proper dress by wearing a pantsuit to the evening service. This was the first time a woman had ever attended a service wearing anything other than a dress. Her fashion statements continued when she began wearing a mini skirt and boots. Many of the women of the congregation felt this was not the proper attire for the lady of the manse. But others, like Jennie VanderBrug (the mother of Duane, the pastor in Harlem, and Mel, who attended Community Church), were not bothered at all by Aliceanne's nonconformist attire, and in fact rather liked it.[145] Aliceanne's next offense was to enroll in art school at Wayne State University. This was entirely inappropriate for the pastor's wife. Her job, as everyone knew, was to stay home and support her husband. Her final transgression came when she announced she had landed a job as a high-end interior designer in Grosse Pointe. This led many of the members of The Fort to ask the obvious question: "Aren't we paying the pastor enough?"

The appropriate dress for church became a frequent topic of conversation during Reverend Steen's tenure. Both men's and women's styles were changing. Bellbottom pants and mini-skirts were the style of the day, and men began to wear colored shirts with their dress suits. The colored shirts began showing up at The Fort, and soon all the men would wear them—except on Communion Sunday, when the elders seemed to feel it appropriate to only wear a white shirt. Reverend Steen, not to be outdone by his wife's fashion sense (or, more likely, as a result of it) began wearing bell-bottom pants to preach in on Sunday. Things were changing at The Fort.

My parents had a difficult time with the ministry of Reverend Steen. I suspect they were more comfortable with the safety of Reverend Groenewold, although he left soon after our arrival in Grosse Pointe and so did not have a big influence on our family. My mother would often say, "He [Steen] is very good with the sick," as if she was trying her best to find something positive to say about him. My Dad found Reverend Steen's sermons to be inconsistent. Some he thought were very good. Others Dad believed showed lack of proper study and preparation during the previous week.

The problem was Reverend Steen did most of his studying in the living room, in a big yellow chair close to his family. His children, of course, would often have the television on, which did not bother Reverend Steen in the slightest. Television really didn't interest him. However, when people would come to the parsonage and see the pastor in the living room with the television on, the story would spread throughout the congregation that he sat home watching TV all day and really didn't work very hard. To my father working hard was the greatest virtue of all. Frank Steen's poor work ethic was reinforced by two incontestable pieces of evidence: the black and white clock on the side wall did not always hit 7 o'clock before he was finished with the evening message, and he began to regularly refer to Archie Bunker during the morning message.

Archie Bunker, of course, was the lead character on the *All in the Family* television show, played by Carroll O'Conner. *All in the Family* was a sit-com featuring the bigoted Bunker, a working-class White male living in Queens, New York, and his equally narrow-minded Polish son-in-law Michael— "Meathead" (played by Rob Reiner). The program aired at 9 p.m. on Saturday evening, and along with most of the members of The Fort and the rest of America, my family would gather around our Magnavox television set and laugh guiltily at the antics of Archie, Edith (Jean Stapleton, the "Dingbat"), daughter Gloria (Sally Struthers) and, of course, George Jefferson (Sherman Hemsley) the equally bigoted Black neighbor. Was it appropriate for a pastor to use such material from the pulpit? Such a question was never raised, and the relevance of the program to the church's struggle with social issues was not fully appreciated. The criticism was simply that Reverend Steen obviously didn't prepare his sermons ahead of time. The truth is, Reverend Steen's mind was mulling over his sermons all week. He would mount the pulpit with only a few note cards, and for the most part speak from his photographic memory. It was not uncommon for something one of the children said on the short walk across the driveway from the parsonage to the church to find its way into the morning message.[146] This led to messages that sometimes appeared rather disorganized and disjointed.

The other place from the entertainment industry that Reverend Steen found sermonic material was the rock-opera *Jesus Christ Superstar*. This was never an issue in my family, but was clearly troublesome to others in the congregation. The idea of using rock-and-roll music to tell the life of Christ was blasphemous enough; but in *Jesus Christ Superstar* there was no resurrection. His critics seemed to overlook the fact that Reverend Steen pointed this out regularly as a shortcoming of the work.

In fact, changes in music were a big concern at The Fort. Prior to Reverend Steen, everyone understood what proper church music was. The prelude and postlude were often written by Bach, taken from Handel's *Messiah* during the Advent, Christmas and Lenten seasons, or from some other Classical composer. To this day, whenever I hear *Sheep May Safely Graze* or *Jesu, Joy of Man's Desiring* I sense a call to worship and in my mind's eye return to The Fort and that beautiful pipe organ. During Reverend Steen's tenure, a whole new genre of Christian music appeared. Some publishing company named "Singspiration" published a spiral-bound, paperback songbook entitled *The Folk Hymnal*. Included with the regular music on the staff were guitar chords, and the young people began to learn guitar and sing these new songs during the youth group meetings. The classic song of this period was entitled "Pass it On."

*It only takes a spark*
*To get a fire going*
*And soon all those around*
*Can warm up in its glowing*
*That's how it is with God's love*
*Once you've experienced it*
*You spread His love to ev'ryone*
*You want to pass it on.*

*What a wondrous time is spring*
*When all the trees are budding*
*The birds begin to sing*
*The flowers start their blooming*
*That's how it is with God's love*
*Once you've experienced it*
*You want to sing it's fresh like spring*

*You want to pass it on*

*I wish for you my friend*
*This happiness that I've found*
*You can depend on Him*
*It matters not where you're bound*
*I'll shout it from the mountain top*
*I want my world to know*
*The Lord of love has come to me*
*I want to pass it on.*[147]

Such songs were fully acceptable at Youth Group meetings but caused some real conflict one Sunday in late summer when they showed up in morning worship. The High School Youth (I was in Junior High at the time and watched all this with fascination from the pew) were led by the Steens, and a number of them began experimenting with the drugs that were common in that day. Over the summer they attended a church camp and for a number of them their faith became very real. The conservative Protestant term for such an experience was that they "got saved." In the terminology of the late 1960's, they stopped getting high on drugs and started getting high on Jesus. When they wanted to share their newfound faith with the congregation, they were invited to do so on a Sunday morning during the worship service. A number of them got up and gave testimonies of their experiences, after which they all joined together in song. The songs they sang that Sabbath morning were taken from *The Folk Hymnal*, accompanied by their guitars. The testimonies brought tears to the eyes of many of the older members of the congregation, who longed more than anything else for the younger generation to embrace the Christian faith. But guitars in church were outside their comfort zone. The guitar was an instrument used on the stage by Rock and Roll singers, who were often dressed in sexually provocative clothing and singing those songs that glorified sex and drugs. How could such an instrument be used to worship Almighty God?

The Fort was not an easy church to pastor, but it was a loving church. The congregation especially loved the youth, and somehow managed from that morning on to from time to time accommodate instruments other than organ and piano in Sunday worship.

The diversity of thinking and perspective among the members of The Fort was a challenge for the pastors, but it was also a challenge for me as a young man growing up in that environment and knowing that I would someday to be a pastor. I would regularly hear the message from my parents, "Pastors are always being criticized." This would often come on a Sunday morning after church, after they had expressed their criticisms of Reverend Steen. This confused me. Is it good to criticize the pastor or not? I suspect they were subtly trying to steer me to a profession other than the ministry. My Dad had no idea what such a life would entail, and was concerned about what he perceived as ministers, such as Reverend Steen, not working very hard.

But my confusion over my parents' criticisms of the pastor was not just over whether or not it was appropriate. Many of the things they disliked about Reverend Steen I found attractive. The pastor would speak about social issues from the pulpit. Unlike my Dad, he would have whole-heartedly agreed with the Grosse Pointe Ministerial Statement of 1966:

> Every person has the moral as well as the legal right to purchase or rent a house anywhere without limitations based on race, color, religion, or national origin. *The churches and their members should lead the way* [italics added] in making sure that

this right of every person is not violated in our own community either by accepted practices or community prejudices.

Reverend Steen understood that the concept of justice is a religious issue deeply embedded in the Hebrew and Christian scriptures. He recognized that Social Justice is as central to the Biblical message as individual salvation. Reverend Steen was ahead of his time. The Christian Reformed Church and The Fort were just beginning to wrestle with the meaning of the Biblical call for Justice. My Dad struggled with this message. He believed Reverend Steen was no longer preaching the "true Gospel," but was preaching the "Social Gospel," which he believed was the message that the Liberal churches were preaching.

The Social Gospel was a response of the Mainline, more liberal Protestant churches to the social issues of the late nineteenth century, especially poverty and the rise of slums as the nation began to urbanize. Protestant pastors became increasingly concerned about the conditions created by industrialization, including overcrowding, the disparity of wealth, and the dehumanization of work in the factory. They rejected Social Darwinism, which explained all these concerns with the phrase "survival of the fittest," and called for a Christianity that included not just an intellectual assent to doctrinal teaching but living a life patterned after the life of Jesus.

Charles M. Sheldon wrote a book that captured this vision, entitled *In His Steps: What Would Jesus Do?* First published in 1896, the book tells the story of Reverend Henry Maxwell, the pastor of the First Church of Raymond, a railroad town in the eastern part of the country. One Friday, while Reverend Maxwell was finishing his sermon, he was interrupted by a hobo seeking help. Not wanting to lose his concentration on the upcoming Sunday's message, Reverend Maxwell quickly escorted the impoverished man out of the building. Two days later the hobo returned during the morning service and stood before the shocked congregation. He criticized the congregation for their apathy and lack of compassion toward poor people like himself, and then passed out. He died a few days later.

Reverend Maxwell responded to these events by doing some deep soul-searching. The following Sunday he preached a sermon in which he challenged the congregation "Do not do anything without first asking, 'What would Jesus do?'" The rest of the book tells what happened when the church members begin asking this question before making major decisions.

*In His Steps* has sold more than 50 million copies. I received two copies of the book for my eighth-grade graduation from Grosse Pointe Christian Day School. I believe one copy was given to me by my parents. I remember my Dad telling me he had read it as a young man and it made a deep impression on him. I do not remember who gave me the other copy. I loved the book. It reinforced my growing sensitivity to the Christian calling to minister with compassion to those who were needy. Nearly thirty years later, while on a trip to Kansas City for training in suicide prevention, I took a side trip to Topeka to visit Central Congregational Church, the church Charles Sheldon pastored while writing the book. I was deeply moved to stand in the pulpit where this great man preached. I was saddened to discover that the staff of the church on duty that day knew little of the significance of their church and its former pastor in American religious history.

Ironically, one hundred years later Evangelical (conservative) Christians discovered once again the phrase central to Sheldon's book. The question, "what would Jesus do?" was reduced to four letters,

WWJD, and sold in conservative Christian bookstores on bracelets and other forms of jewelry. I suspect few of those who purchased these trinkets and proudly wore them knew of the connection to Sheldon's book and the "liberal" Social Gospel movement.

Social Gospel moved the focus of the Christian faith from individual belief to the character of Jesus Christ. For pastors influenced by the Social Gospel, it was not enough to follow the first of Jesus' Great Commandments, "Love God above all." Authentic Christianity required following the second Great Commandment, "Love your neighbor as yourself" (See Matthew 22:37-39). The pursuit of Social Justice was seen as an outworking of Christian faith.

In contrast with the Social Gospel movement, Dwight M. Moody focused his energies on the salvation of individual souls. For Moody, society could only change if individual souls were changed. According to Moody, it was the immorality of the poor that led to their poverty, especially the sins of laziness, a lack of thrift, and the consumption of liquor and tobacco. Such sins inevitably led to poverty. Moody understood laziness and idleness to be particularly heinous sins. The pastor's job, according to Moody, was to preach the gospel and save souls. "Don't have anything to say about capital and labor. You don't know anything about it. . . What right have you to criticize President Cleveland? You had better preach the gospel and let him deal with questions of state about which you know nothing."[148] The theology of Dwight M. Moody continues to have a strong influence in American Fundamentalism.

The Social Gospel movement and the Fundamentalism of Dwight M. Moody. Two American religious developments of the late 19th Century, during the Progressive Era in American history.

Meanwhile, in the Netherlands, two groups broke away from the Dutch Reformed Church in the nineteenth century, roughly paralleling the Social Gospel and Moody's Fundamentalism in America. Both groups had a strong influence on the CRC and on The Fort.

The first group was the *Afgescheidenen*, "Separatists," who seceded from the Dutch Reformed Church in 1834. Albertus Van Raalte and Dirk Eppinga were part of this group before they moved to America. The *Afgescheidenen* were primarily from the north and were poor farmers. Like the Fundamentalism of Dwight M. Moody, theirs was a very simple faith, more concerned with personal piety and godliness than deep theology.

The second group left the mother church in 1886, under the leadership of Reverend Abraham Kuyper. Kuyper began his ministry in the small village church of Beesd, but soon moved on to serve churches in Utrecht and Amsterdam, both urban centers. The Utrecht congregation, with 35,000 members, and the congregation in Amsterdam, with 140,000 members 28 ministers, 10 sanctuaries, and four chapels, is quite a contrast to the rural origin and character of the *Afgescheidenen*.

In 1885 Kuyper and the Consistory (the full church board including elders, deacons, and pastor) of the church in Amsterdam began requiring both officers and members of his church to agree with the three Reformed Confessions: The Heidelberg Catechism, the Belgic Confession of Faith, and the Canons of Dordt. His and the Consistory's concern was a perceived lack of Reformed distinctiveness in the state-run Dutch Reformed Church. Members of the congregation appealed this decision of the Consistory to the Classis (regional body of churches), which suspended both Kuyper and the Consistory. A further appeal to the Provincial Synod (higher body) upheld the ruling of Classis. Kuyper and his followers withdrew from the Dutch Reformed Church, as did a number of congregations that agreed with him. Those who left became known as the *Dolerenden*, from the Latin word *dolere*, "'to feel sorrow." These were the "grieving ones," saddened at the perceived loss of Reformed distinctiveness and orthodoxy in the Dutch Reformed Church. In 1892 Kuyper and his Grieving Ones joined the Separatists to form the Reformed Churches in the Netherlands (*Gereformeerde kerk*). The Christian Reformed Church was the American version of the Reformed Churches in the Netherlands, while the Reformed Church in America (RCA), the denomination Dirk Eppinga was admonished not to join, is the American version of the Dutch Reformed Church (*Nederlands Hervormde Kerk*).

Unlike the Separatists, who tended to withdraw from society, Kuyper believed in social engagement. In 1874 he was elected to the Dutch legislature and resigned his position as a pastor of the church in Amsterdam. As both a pastor and a politician, Kuyper was concerned with the social problems caused by the Industrial Revolution, including economic inequality, poverty, and inhumane working conditions. In 1891, five years before Charles M. Sheldon wrote *In His Steps: What Would Jesus Do,* Kuyper gave a speech entitled *The Problem of Poverty* to the First Christian Social Congress held in the Netherlands. In that speech Kuyper said, "It is so profoundly false that God's Word lets us hear only calls for the salvation of our souls. No, God's Word gives us firm ordinances—even for our national existence and our common social life."[149] Seven years later Kuyper, in a speech at Princeton Seminary on the American side of the Atlantic Ocean, once again spoke of the necessity of Christians to be involved in society. "Instead of monastic flight *from* the world," he told his Princeton audience, "the duty [of the

144

Christian] is now emphasized of serving God *in* the world, in every position in life."[150]

The American immigrants who came from the Separatist farmers resonated with the personal piety and simple teaching of Dwight M. Moody. The Grieving Ones who immigrated were more in harmony with the Social Gospel movement.

My Dad was very perceptive. Reverend Steen was in fact preaching a version of the Social Gospel, a Dutch Reformed version which was strongly influenced by Abraham Kuyper. Kuyper was no liberal—his concern for doctrinal orthodoxy in the Dutch Reformed Church made that clear. Nor was Reverend Steen, a graduate of the Conservative Westminster Seminary in Philadelphia, a liberal. However, both Abraham Kuyper and Frank Steen were deeply concerned about the social problems of their day. "Kuyper . . . (discerned) how Jesus and his teachings applied to the social problems of first-century Palestine. Then Kuyper. . . (took) those lessons and . . . (applied) Jesus' teaching to Dutch society during the Industrial Revolution."[151] Reverend Steen did the very same thing, applying his sermons to the injustice and racial tension of Detroit in the late 1960s. The sermons that made the most impact on me were not his conservative, doctrinal sermons often based on the Book of Romans, where Reverend Steen explained Christian dogma. The sermons that found fertile soil in my young heart were the sermons about Jesus. Sermons about how the humble carpenter from Galilee treated the sick and the needy.

These sermons not only showed the influence of Abraham Kuyper, but also the influence of an American preacher, a preacher who also had a Doctorate, a preacher who was also highly influenced by the Social Gospel movement.[152] That preacher's name was Doctor Martin Luther King, Jr. A little more than a year after Reverend Steen came to Detroit,

Doctor King spoke at Grosse Pointe High School. That story will be the subject of Chapter Eight.

The CRC in the 1960s had both Separatists and Grieving Ones within her membership. My Dad was a Separatist, deeply concerned with personal piety and individual salvation. Frank Steen was a Grieving One, deeply moved, not by doctrinal laxity, but by the brokenness of the city in which he had been called to serve. I was a young boy, carefully taking in the teachings of these two spiritual giants. Family loyalty meant I had to follow my Dad's Separatist ways. But the constant exposure to both the affluence of Grosse Pointe and the poverty of the declining city of Detroit had made an impact on me. I grieved over the conditions in which the Black community of Detroit were forced to live. I wept at the funeral of Dr. Martin Luther King, Jr. I was in fact a Grieving One, grieving over the broken state of the city and the injustice I saw all around me. As I moved through my teenage years, I grew increasingly confused, angry, and depressed.

The Fort was not an easy church to pastor with the diversity of thinking and perspective among its members. Times were changing in both society and the church, and this was as challenging and exciting for Frank Steen as it was difficult. When he received a call to Sioux Center, Iowa no one, including his family, thought he would move. Reverend Steen loved Detroit, and the people of The Fort loved him. But, surprisingly, after eight years in Detroit, he did accept the call and moved to Iowa.

Sometimes when Frank Steen was sitting on the porch steps with Jim Groenewold and drinking beer, he would ask the Vietnam War Veteran how his father dealt with the challenges of pastoring The Fort. John Groenewold the *Dominee* and Frank Steen in bellbottom pants both faced the same challenges. Frank's success was a direct result of his mild manner. He never pushed for his own views, which was unusual in a church full of people pushing their divergent views.[153] One Sunday morning following a few weeks of vacation, Reverend Steen appeared in the pulpit sporting a beard. One of the conservative members of The Fort complained to him about it on the way out. By the evening service, the beard was gone. Reverend Steen knew the importance of picking his battles carefully.

One battle Reverend Steen picked came at the very beginning of his tenure at The Fort. Three weeks after he was installed as pastor, Detroit experienced the worst race riots in the nation's history. Reverend Steen believed the church needed to respond in a tangible way, and for him the proper response was obvious: the Grosse Pointe Christian Day School, located behind The Fort, needed to be integrated.

*"The rich need the poor.  Otherwise they lose their souls."*

-Joel Van Ornum

*"The struggle. . .has made us ask ourselves about our Christian faith, its nature and demands."*

-Reverend Duane VanderBrug

# Chapter 7

# Integrating a Christian School

The Grosse Pointe Christian Day School (GPCDS), attached to the back of The Fort, violated all the conventional wisdom of how to run a successful school. The facilities were sub-par: a forty-year-old building with four classrooms serving eight grades on the main floor, the bathrooms, an all-purpose room, and a kitchen in the basement (which was prone to flooding). The small playground was equipped with a few swings and a set of monkey bars. The paved church parking lot served as a ball field. The school was understaffed: four full-time teachers each responsible for two grades. The Junior High teacher, Mr. Jonker, also served as the principle. Three part-time teachers, one for Junior High English and history, one for art, and one for music. All underpaid by any reasonable assessment. When the telephone rang, one of the students in the Junior High class would run out of the classroom, down the hall and up a flight of stairs to the teacher's lounge and, breathless from the mini-marathon, manage to recite the script he or she had been taught: "This is a Grosse Pointe Christian Day School student speaking. May I help you?" Every other Friday we had "hot lunch," (if the basement wasn't flooded), the proceeds of which went to provide funds that went back into improvements for the school.

I cannot imagine a better education than the one I received at Grosse Pointe Christian.

The fifth largest city in the country was our classroom. At least once a year the Detroit Symphony would have a special program for children. On those occasions a chartered bus from the Lakeshore Bus

Line—one of those outdated 1950s models with the rounded corners—would arrive in front of The Fort. We would climb aboard—four grades fit easily on one bus—for the drive down Jefferson Avenue to the Ford Theater. Once inside and seated comfortably we would be bored by the music for one to two hours. The professional musicians would explain what was going on, but somehow, I don't remember anything they said. Our family owned a record— what would later be referred to as a vinyl—of Prokofiev's "Peter and the Wolf," which was far more effective than the Detroit Symphony in teaching me about orchestral music.

The Art teacher, Mrs. Wassenaar, was more effective in instilling in me an appreciation for classical art. We were supposed to work on art projects ourselves, which wasn't something I was particularly good at. It was the lessons on the great artists of history that made a lasting impression in me. Of course, the Dutch Masters, especially the Calvinist Rembrandt with his dark colors, were the epitome of fine art. But we also learned about Monet, Picasso, and more contemporary artists, always illustrated with pictures of their works hanging in the Detroit Institute of Arts. From time to time that same Lakeshore Bus Line coach would arrive to take us to the Detroit Institute of Arts to see the originals.

Our school didn't have a library of its own. The Park branch of the Grosse Pointe Public Library was our library. Every class made the bi-weekly six-block hike to the library where the librarians exposed us to children's writers such as Laura Ingalls Wilder and Marguerite Henry. They explained the meaning of the gold seals on a few of the books, which indicated they had won the Newberry Prize for children's books and were therefore especially good. They taught us the Dewey Decimal system and how to use the card catalogue. The visits began with our returning the books we had previously checked out and ended with browsing through the stacks and choosing new books to check out.

Our history teacher was Mrs. Dunn, the wife of a local Presbyterian minister, a staunch Republican, and oblivious to any modern methods of education. Her style included a heavy dose of reading and written answers to questions reproduced on mimeographed papers. We memorized the Declaration of Independence and the Preamble to the Constitution, learned not only about the Boston Tea Party and the Civil War, but also about the Articles of Confederation, the Whiskey Rebellion, the Missouri Compromise, and Manifest Destiny. She did include one rather creative experience in her pedagogy. There were a number of historical markers in Downtown Detroit pointing out significant locations from the past. One sunny afternoon in the spring the Lakeshore Bus arrived and took us downtown. We stood in the spot where some French guy named Cadillac built a fort that he called Fort Pontchartrain. Prior to this advancement in my education I had thought Cadillac was someone who either built a car or founded a city in northern Michigan, and that Pontchartrain, the name of one of the exclusive hotels downtown, was the name of a hotel baron like Hilton or Weston. On that trip we walked inside a number of historically important churches, some of which sold post cards in the foyer with pictures of the building and its windows. I was horrified. Selling postcards in church was a direct violation of Jesus' teaching in reaction to the moneychangers in the temple. The church that made the biggest impression on me was the Mariner's Church. The story of people coming across the ocean from Europe and using the wood from their ship to build a church challenged my imagination.

The adults were concerned that the curriculum was weak in the sciences. They really didn't have to worry, as our teachers were amazingly creative and used every opportunity available to teach. On those walks to the Library we went down Nottingham Avenue, where many of the trees were dying from something called Dutch Elm disease. Watching the bi-weekly ritual of tree cutters taking down yet another dead tree and gradually transforming Nottingham Avenue from a beautiful tree-lined street to a sunny road with a row of saplings on either side planted between the pavement and the sidewalk taught valuable lessons in biology and ecology. But the adults were concerned, and since they did not have the resources to outfit an entire room as a laboratory, they settled for a "Science table" that could be wheeled from room to room. This table came equipped with a sink that used potable water, beakers, petri dishes, and a Bunsen burner. Plenty of opportunities for experiments for our Junior High classes. The adults then decided that we needed to have a "Science Camp." This was a wonderful week in May when we would all go by a chartered Lakeshore bus to Proud Lake near Wixom. Mr. Jonker would scoop up swamp water and show us amoebas under the microscope, we would take walks and identify the various plants and animals (including snakes) that could be found in Michigan, and most importantly for our Science education, we would spend hours swimming in the lake.

But the most powerful lessons I learned at Grosse Pointe Christian Day School were about race.

Although the Christian School was on the same property as The Fort and the two buildings were connected, people were quick to point out that the school was not a parochial school. Parochial schools, like Lutheran or Catholic schools, were run by the church. In Christian Reformed thinking, Christian Schools were to be operated by the parents who were members of a school society rather than the church. Operating

Christian Schools was a tangible way for the faithful to live out their beliefs. In the case of The Fort and the Grosse Pointe Christian School, it would take a skilled lawyer to tell the difference between a parochial and a parent run school. Almost all of the students came from families that were members of The Fort. The offering envelopes for The Fort included a place where members could designate a part of their weekly offerings for the school, and special offerings were regularly taken for the school. But the distinction was there and was particularly important to the members of The Fort.

How to live out their faith became a real challenge beginning with the June 1967 School Board meeting, just one month before the rebellion. At that meeting the School Board President, Mr. Van de Riet, made a report to the Board about another meeting held six days earlier on June 22. A copy of the minutes of this earlier meeting had been submitted to each member prior to the board meeting to acquaint them with the action being contemplated. According to the Board minutes, after Mr. Van de Riet's report "A long discussion was held on the subject during which each board member expressed his feelings on the matter."

The unnamed subject that was arousing board members' feelings was the possibility of admitting Black children from the Community Christian Reformed Church as students to the school. [154]

The Board members feelings about the possibility of integrating the Christian School were understandable. This was less than a year after Gordon Wright bought his home in Grosse Pointe Woods. The Wrights had moved out of Grosse Pointe the previous November, but the issue of race relations in Grosse Pointe was still sensitive. In March, Grosse Pointe once again made national news as an exclusively White community. An estimated 18 million television viewers saw a report of the failed integration efforts in Grosse Pointe on the Huntley-Brinkley Report. Grosse Pointe continued to be a national symbol of racial segregation.

Additionally, the issue of school integration was a sensitive one. In 1954 the Supreme Court ruled unanimously in the case of *Brown vs. the Board of Education* that racial segregation in public schools was unconstitutional and called on district courts and school boards to implement desegregation "with all deliberate speed." This one ruling completely undermined Court's the earlier ruling in *Plessy vs. Ferguson* (1896), where the Court ruled that "separate but equal" public facilities were constitutional. *Plessy* was the legal ground for the Jim Crow laws. The *Brown* decision was resisted, and in 1957 President Eisenhower sent federal troops to Little Rock, Arkansas, to protect nine students—the "Little Rock Nine"—in their attempt to attend Central High School. Closer to home, the segregation continued in Detroit. As we saw earlier, Northern High School twelve miles away had an all-Black student body. The Grosse Pointe system had an all-White student body—and an all-White faculty.

Two months before Mr. Van de Riet brought the subject of integration up to the Board of Grosse Pointe Christian, eight hundred students and faculty of Grosse Pointe High School signed a letter "to Students of Education at Michigan Colleges and Universities" encouraging "any student or graduate, regardless of religion or race, to apply to teach at our school." According to the letter,

> ...as the faculty here comes to include more people of varied backgrounds, the normal give-and-take of school and community life will create more opportunities for developing natural attitudes and comfortable human relationships. As students, we have a particular interest in this, because we want to be able to

take our places responsibly and effectively in a world where White people comprise less than a third of the population.[155]

At least four of the signers of the letter were members of The Fort and alumni of Grosse Pointe Christian: Mary Schaafsma, Debbie Niewhouse, Pat Dykstra and Barbara Feikens. This is a rather significant number when one considers how few such students there were at Grosse Pointe High School.

But there was something else that was undoubtedly behind the Board members' feelings about the possibility of integrating the Christian School, something going on not in Grosse Pointe or Detroit, but in Chicago, 300 miles to the west. Two years earlier, in 1965, a request came to the executive committee of the Timothy Christian School Board, in the western suburb of Cicero, similar to the request now before the Board of Grosse Pointe Christian. The request came from the pastor of the Lawndale CRC, a predominately Black congregation in Chicago, to admit 21 Black students to the Timothy Christian School. The committee members agreed not to accept the students. Their concern was that the presence of these students would result in violence.

The Committee had good reason for such concern. Cicero was a working-class community known for racial intolerance. In 1951 the suburb was the site of a race riot when a Black family, the Clarks, moved into one of the apartment buildings in the city. On July 11 of that year, 4,000 Whites attacked the apartment building, destroying not only the Clark apartment but the apartments of the other residents as well. The riot came to an end only after the Illinois governor called in the National Guard.

The executive committee of the Timothy School did agree to appoint a committee to make alternative arrangements for the students from Lawndale. At the next regional meeting of the churches, Classis Chicago North, the delegates from Lawndale church informed the Classis that they were seeking Christian School education for their children and had been denied such education by the Timothy Christian School Board. Soon the Board began receiving letters asking if racism was involved. Students at Calvin College, the denomination's school in Grand Rapids, MI, reported on the issue in the student newspaper, *Chimes*: "The school board justified its refusal of the Lawndale parent's request on the grounds that the community in which the school was located could be hostile to the presence of these children in their city. The cause of the refusal . . . the children are Black." Articles were written on the issue in the CRC denominational paper, *The Banner*. Eventually the matter was taken to court in October 1971. The issue was finally resolved when Timothy Christian School closed its Cicero campus and consolidated operations in nearby Elmhurst, which was more open to the presence of Black students.[156]

The men on the Grosse Pointe Christian School Board were undoubtedly aware of the situation in Lawndale and Cicero. The Lawndale Church had recently installed a new pastor, Reverend Duane VanderBrug, the brother of Mel VanderBrug from the Community Church in Detroit. Duane grew up attending The Fort and was an alumnus of Grosse Pointe Christian School. Duane and Mel's mother, Jennie, was a charter member of The Fort and very influential. A third brother, Gordon, was married to the third and fourth grade teacher at Grosse Pointe Christian. These personal connections almost certainly influenced the Grosse Pointe School Board members' attitude and final decision.

After the Board members expressed their feelings, Mr. Van de Reit asked the Education Committee to look into the matter of teacher attitudes and pupil testing and asked the Finance Committee to investigate the possible financial concerns and report back at the July 26 Board meeting. No meeting was held on July 26, 1967 because of the rioting going on. The rebellion likely intensified the struggle in the Board member's hearts about whether or not to admit African American children to the Christian School in Grosse Pointe.

One of the teachers contacted by the Education Committee was the fifth and sixth grade teacher, Shirley Verspoor. Shirley was personally aware of the need, but also of the hostility between the races in Detroit at the time. Her husband, Carl, was a law student at Wayne State University. During the summer months she would catch a ride downtown with her husband when he had to attend class and would volunteer at the Community Church as a tutor. On other occasions she would take the bus. There were two bus lines available to her at the time. The buses operated by the City of Detroit were green, while the private Lakeshore Coach line had red and silver buses. The Lakeshore line made no stops between Grosse Pointe and downtown, while the Detroit buses ran down Mack Avenue alongside Grosse Pointe and continued making stops every few blocks until it reached downtown. Since money was tight, she took the Detroit bus, saving 50 cents in bus fare. She was often the only White person on the bus, which at first did not bother her. However, one day when she was the only White passenger someone grabbed her purse. "I need help," she called out. No one came to her aid. From then on, she spent the extra 50 cents for the suburban bus.

The Education Committee did as they were assigned and informed Shirley Verspoor and the other teachers that the Board was thinking about admitting students from the Community Church. The teachers' response was positive. They understood the challenge of getting the Black children up to grade level, understood that if they took on this extra work the Board would not be able to increase their pay, but they also had a heart for the Black children of the Community Church. The teachers responded that they were willing to take on this challenge. Deep down the teachers didn't think it would ever happen.[157]

Shirley Verspoor made it a priority the following school year to prepare her students for the possible integration of the school. I was in her 5th grade class that year and remember well—and was forever impacted by—her efforts. She began the first day of school by reading/telling us a Bible Story we had never heard before:

> One day the trees went out to anoint a king for themselves. They said to the olive tree, "Be our king."
> But the olive tree answered, "Should I give up my oil, by which both gods and humans are honored, to hold sway over the trees?"
> Next, the trees said to the fig tree, "Come and be our king."
> But the fig tree replied, "Should I give up my fruit, so good and sweet, to hold sway over the trees?"
> Then the trees said to the vine, "Come and be our king."
> But the vine answered, "Should I give up my wine, which cheers both gods and humans, to hold sway over the trees?"
> Finally, all the trees said to the thornbush, "Come and be our king."
> The thornbush said to the trees, "If you really want to anoint me king over you, come and take refuge in my shade."
>
> -Judges 9:8-15

The lesson she gleaned from this story was about the value of both diversity and individuality. We students might be different from each other, but each of us brings something that is of value to all.

The lessons went on that year and got more specific. When dismissing the class for recess, she would dismiss the blue-eyed children first, making those with brown eyes wait. On another day she would dismiss children who had tied shoes, insisting that those with Velcro ties remain in their seats. She then led class discussions on how we felt being picked out and given second-rate status based on something as arbitrary as our eye color or the kind of shoes we wore that morning. She compared that to skin color, which she explained was an arbitrary feature and ought not be used to use to treat people differently.[158]

The most powerful lessons I learned at Grosse Pointe Christian Day School were about race.

The next board meeting was held on August 30, one month after the rebellion. "A report was received for information concerning the negro [sic] children from Community Chr Ref Church entering our school. The decision to [sic] entering our school is being considered for the 68-69 session after Rev Botts of the Community Chr Ref Church has conducted proper testing with the perspective students."[159] During that meeting the Board also dealt with a member who thought that a $600 pledge was required to admit his children to the school. The Board agreed that this was not correct, that no covenant child would be refused a Christian education because of monetary considerations."[160]

The concept of "covenant children" was an important one to the Board. A "covenant child" is the child of a believer, of a member of the church community. According to the Heidelberg Catechism, "Infants as well as adults are included in God's covenant and people."[161] Because of this, they should be baptized, and are to be "distinguished from the children of unbelievers."[162] The church believed it had a special responsibility toward these children, as they took a vow at the children's baptisms to train them in the Christian faith. Christian Day School education was a major and concrete way the church kept this vow. This concept of covenant children would play a key part in the Board's final decision about African American students.

At their Sept. 27 meeting the board decided to invite Reverend Botts to meet with them and "discuss the problems incident to having Negro children entering our school."[163] One of the concerns once again raised by the board was the financial implication of admitting the students. The "suggestion was made. . . [to] check into federal subsidies for Negro children entering parochial schools under the General Welfare clauses of the Federal Government."[164] Reverend Botts met with the Board on November 29, along with Dave Cooke and Mel VanderBrug representing the two families from the Grosse Pointe church that attended the Community Church on a weekly basis. According to the minutes, the board's concerns centered on three things:

> A. It was the feeling that educational standards would not and could not be compromised and that negro [sic] parents must be made fully aware of this.
> B. Concerning tuition and cost of education the Board would be most helpful—but basically this is a parental responsibility.
> C. There is a defined need for a process of education for our present Christian School constituency to facilitate the acceptance of Negro children in our school.[165]

Throughout the entire process the Board seemed to be struggling with the question: "How do we get to 'Yes' in answer to this request?"

Across town things were different. At the January 31 meeting Board members were informed by Dr. Phil Feringa (who by this time had replaced Mr. Van de Riet as board president): "Dearborn is out as far as educating Negro children."[166] The reference is undoubtedly to the Dearborn Christian School, affiliated with the Dearborn Christian Reformed Church. The Dearborn school had also received a request from the Community Church to admit their children. But Dearborn was a blue-collar community nationally known for its racist mayor, Orville Hubbard. Mayor Hubbard was once quoted as saying he was "for complete segregation, one million percent."[167] It is likely the Board of the Dearborn Christian School had many of the same fears as the Timothy Christian School in Cicero.[168]

The work of preparing for African American students to be admitted to the Grosse Pointe School continued. The Board was concerned about the attitude of the broader Grosse Pointe Christian School constituency and took proactive steps to facilitate the constituency's acceptance of Black students to the School. At the April 24, 1968 meeting, board member John Batts (who four years earlier had donated his time and carpentry skills to helping turn the basement of the Community Church into a sanctuary) was given the responsibility of devising "a questionnaire to help determine the reaction of the people of the school society to the Community Church children entering our school."[169] The results were discussed "in detail" at the following meeting.[170]

At the May 29, 1968 meeting a final decision had to be made. "A letter was read from the parents of the Community Christian Reformed Church making applications for 11 children to the Grosse Pointe Christian School."[171] Rather than the 25 students identified by Reverend

Botts on November 29, the letter included only children at the fourth-grade level and below. This was likely a concession to the concern for academic standards and the difficulty of bringing older students up to grade level. The decision was clearly a difficult one for the Board, and the members did not make it lightly.

A two one-half hour discussion ensued in which scholastic standings were discussed. It was brought out that a difficulty would be the children's short attention span, but it was felt that this was a correctible situation. The possibility of starting a Community Christian School was discussed but it was considered inadvisable and unworkable. The questionnaires sent to the School Society members were also discussed in detail. A motion was then made and supported to accept the covenant children from the inner-city on the same basis as children from other backgrounds based on the conditions set forth by the School Board and applicatory letter.[172]

It is important to note the way the motion was worded. These may have been "Negro" children, but the board saw them first and foremost as "covenant" children. They had been baptized. They were to be "distinguished from the children of unbelievers." What distinguished these children was not their skin color, but their baptism. GPCDS was a school for "covenant" children, and the Board believed as indicated by their earlier decision that "no covenant child would be refused a Christian education because of monetary considerations."

The vote was taken by secret ballot. The results were unanimous. The Board members had no choice but to vote "yes," based on their deeply held theological convictions. The decision was made on principle, and the result was stunning: The predominately Dutch Christian School in Grosse Pointe was open to Black students.[173]

162

Since the vote was unanimous, my Dad obviously voted to open the Christian School to Black students. He voted in a secret ballot to put his children at whatever risk was required to allow Black Covenant Children the opportunity for a Christian School education. There is nothing my Dad has done in his entire life that makes me prouder of him than that very difficult vote.

A letter was immediately sent to the school's constituency informing them of the Board's decision, and discussion was held the following month at the annual School Society meeting. The Chairman answered some questions from the floor "which were concerned with educational standards, monetary support and community reactions relative to the children from Community Christian Reformed Church entering our School."[174]

There is no indication in the minutes that there was any serious opposition to admitting Black children to the school; no indication that there were any threats by Society members to withdraw their support if the Community children were admitted. The members of the Society seem to be of one mind that race was not to be a factor in considering who would be admitted to "their" school.

And so, in September 1968, fourteen months after the Detroit riots, a rusty, second hand, yellow school bus with eleven Black children crossed Altar Road and entered Grosse Pointe, dropping the students off at the predominately Dutch Christian School. Reverend Steen's goal of responding to the riots in a tangible way was met. Once again, it was the churches of Grosse Pointe—this time the conservative, Dutch church in the shadow of Altar and Mack—that led the way in the pursuit of civil rights. While it was the Mainline Churches—Unitarian, Episcopalian, and Presbyterian—that took the lead in open housing, The Fort took the lead in breaking the color line in the area of education.

The main question remaining was how the community surrounding The Fort would respond. This had been the concern of the Timothy Christian School Board in Cicero, outside Chicago. It was likely the concern of the Dearborn Christian School board on the west side of the city when they chose not to accept students from Community Church. How would the community of Grosse Pointe react? Would the response be one of acceptance, as was exhibited by the marchers walking down Kercheval Avenue accompanied by Governor Romney in June of 1963? Or would the response include harassment, like the Gordon Wright's received when they moved into Grosse Pointe Woods? Would it be something worse? The school bus was well used and looked it. The children came from homes that were far less affluent than the Wrights. This was not the image Grosse Pointers wanted to maintain for their community. What would be the response?

The Board sent two letters to community leaders that summer informing them of their decision. Board Secretary, Curtis Vrieland, sent a letter to the Mayor of Grosse Pointe Park and to the Grosse Pointe Human Relations Committee formally informing them of the acceptance of the Community children to the school.[175] Board member Robert Melling was tasked with giving "a resume to the Grosse Pointe Human Relations Committee concerning the children of the Community Church coming to our school,"[176] and reported back to the August board meeting "that the Human Relations Committee of Grosse Pointe will discuss the children from Community Church coming to our school at their Executive Board Meeting."[177] Whether or not the Human Relations Committee actually held that discussion is unknown. There is no confirmation in the records that they did.

The Community did, in fact, react. On more than one occasion the bus was met at the city limits by a group of angry residents who threw rocks. On one occasion one of the bus windows was broken.[178] Although no one was hurt, the children were traumatized when they arrived at school.

This overt racism moved me deeply. Since I was in the sixth grade, none of the Black students were in my classroom, and I never interacted with the traumatized students. But I was fully aware of what was going on, and had a difficult time making sense of it. How could the people of Grosse Pointe be so mean? How could they throw rocks at a bus filled with children? How was the breaking of the windows of the school bus any different than the rioters who threw rocks through the windows of stores a year earlier?

The Christian School was not the first school in Grosse Pointe to be integrated. Two years earlier, the private Grosse Pointe University School admitted its first Black student. At some point *The Detroit News* ran an article that claimed Grosse Pointe University School was the only integrated school in Grosse Pointe. This upset my Dad, who was one of the Christian School's strongest supporters. He wrote a Letter to the Editor saying that GPCDS was also integrated. I remember the letter appearing in print, under the heading "G.P. Christian Is Integrated." I was proud of my Dad for getting his letter printed in the newspaper. Soon after that the telephone rang one evening when I was in charge of babysitting my younger siblings. I answered the phone, and a woman, obviously intoxicated, asked to speak to my father. I informed her, as I was instructed in such situations: "He can't come to the phone right now." She then proceeded to yell at me. "You tell your Nigger loving father . . ." I honestly don't remember the rest of the message, but the call scared me. I'm sure I relayed the message and that was the end of it.

But I knew that there were those in Grosse Pointe who were not happy with the Christian School, my school, including Black students.

But in other ways the people of Grosse Pointe were very supportive, often unaware they were doing so. The Christian School had for years maintained an excellent relationship with the Grosse Pointe Public School System (as, I suspect, did the Catholic Schools in Grosse Pointe). Once a year a woman from the public schools would come to Grosse Pointe Christian to test the students' hearing. Later she would return to test vision. A speech therapist made weekly trips to the school to assist students, including those who had immigrated and had difficulty with certain sounds not used in the Dutch language. And, of course, we made the trips to the Grosse Pointe Public Library, run by the school system. All these services were now available to the Black students from the inner-city of Detroit who were enrolled in the school.

The Black students had their own adjustments to make. Already in August, before the Black students arrived, the school's principal reported to the board that he would "order sample copies of racially and culturally integrated readers for the study of teachers and educational committee members."[179] It was obvious early on that these students had a shorter attention span. Many of them were behind grade level. A number of women from the School Society volunteered to come on a regular basis to tutor these children. Finances were always a problem. Enrollment was falling, and the school had to face some serious financial challenges. When tuition was raised, the Board made special accommodations for the Community Church children, so that they could continue to attend. The Board decided it needed representation from the Community Church and so Mrs. Stevens, the mother of several of the students from Community Church, was chosen to serve as a full member of the board.

She became not only the first African American but also the first woman to serve on the board. Things were changing at The Fort.

Behavior was a constant challenge, especially on the playground. The Board minutes make regular references to students using bad language. One student's disrespect to Mrs. Dunn came to the attention of the Board; the matter appears to have been resolved. Another student pulled a knife on one of my friends, Tom Van Wingerden. That incident scared me. I don't know if this ever came to the attention of the adults. There is no mention of it in the Board minutes.

The most important lessons I learned at Grosse Pointe Christian Day School were about race. But my education was not limited to the school. Reverend Steen, pastor of The Fort, taught me lessons he learned from another pastor, Dr. Martin Luther King, Jr., who spoke to an audience in Grosse Pointe three weeks before he was assassinated in Memphis. Dr. King's story is in the next chapter.

*"Our nation is moving toward two societies, one Black, one White—separate and unequal."*

-Kerner Commission Report, February 29, 1968

*"It was clear that Whites and Blacks had to try to understand each other."*

-Jude Huetteman, Civil Rights Activist from Grosse Pointe[180]

*"Mr. King came, he spoke, and that is that."*

-Zolia F. Allor[181]

# Chapter 8

# Dr. King Comes to Grosse Pointe

Like most Americans my age, I remember where I was when I learned that President Kennedy had been shot. I remember where I was when I heard that the first tower of the World Trade Center had been hit by an airplane. I also remember where I was when I learned that Dr. King was coming to Grosse Pointe.

My Dad drove us to school every morning on his way to work. One morning, while we were at the corner of Littlestone Road and Mack Avenue, just three blocks from home, the news came over the radio. My father was visibly upset. "Why is he coming here to stir up trouble?" he asked to no one in particular. "We are just recovering from the riots. We don't need more trouble."

Dad's response was not an uncommon one in Grosse Pointe. As a member of the Grosse Pointe Christian School Board, he had voted to admit Black students to the school. At the same time, there was a deep fear. The announcement of Dr. King's coming to Grosse Pointe struck that frightened nerve. I understood Dad's fear. I even shared it. But I also had had enough exposure to this Black man, to the impoverished Black community of Detroit that had rioted eight months earlier, and to the fine teaching of Mrs. Verspoor in the Christian School that I could see how important it was for Dr. King to come to Grosse Pointe. I was a conflicted pre-adolescent; many of these conflicts remained with me for most of my life. I did not understand that morning that my Dad's angst and my confusion were a reflection of the entire community's response to the news that Dr. King was coming.

It is difficult for the young reader to understand just how controversial Dr. King was in 1968. Today Dr. King is responsible for a well-needed holiday during the long month of January. Perhaps his best-known accomplishment is probably a speech given on the steps of the Lincoln Memorial, a rather sentimental speech in which he articulates a dream about children of various races.

> I have a dream that my four little children will one day live in a nation where they will not be judged by the color of their skin but by the content of their character. I have a dream today.
>
> I have a dream that one day down in Alabama, with its vicious racists, with its governor having his lips dripping with the words of "interposition" and "nullification," one day right there in Alabama little Black boys and Black girls will be able to join hands with little White boys and White girls as sisters and brothers. I have a dream today.[182]

In fact, that morning when the news report came over the radio, Dr. King was a divisive figure and had been for more than a decade. After the 1955 Montgomery Bus boycott, the FBI began monitoring King's activities. In 1962 Attorney General Robert Kennedy authorized wiretaps on King's home. J. Edgar Hoover, head of the FBI, called King the "most notorious liar in the country" in a November 1964 press conference. A 1965 Gallop poll found 45% of Americans viewed King positively and 45% negatively. King's vocal opposition to the Vietnam War only increased his controversial standing. 64% of Americans supported the war according to a Gallop poll published in 1965. By 1966 King's Gallop poll numbers had dropped significantly: 32% of Americans viewed him positively while 65% viewed him negatively.[183]

Dr. King may have been controversial, but I found him fascinating. My dreams of becoming a missionary in a distant place like Africa had matured over the previous two years into a fascination with that close yet far away world of the African Americans in Detroit. The rebellion made a huge impact on me. A visit to the Community Church with a group from The Fort exposed me to a completely different style of worship. Not only was their music much livelier and filled with more syncopation than the Bach organ music of The Fort, they even sang one of the songs played on CKLW, the top 40 music station out of Windsor. Simon and Garfunkel's *Bridge Over Troubled Water* was one of my favorites. But it didn't seem right, raised as I was in a conservative home, to use it as church music. When I mentioned my concerns to my friend, Tom Van Wingerden, he replied: "Jesus is our Bridge Over Troubled Water." I was not convinced.

Soon after the rebellion one of my classmates in Shirley Verspoor's class wrote a poem about Dr. King. The poet was Dave Cooke, Jr. the young White boy who attended the Community Church. He was, quite frankly, something of a bully. I was one of his victims. But something deeper was stirring in Dave's soul, and as he read the poem, I could sense the deep emotion, something spiritual, which resonated in my own soul. And so, on that late winter morning on the corner of Littlestone Road and Mack Avenue, Dave Cooke's deep pain for the suffering of the poor in Detroit, which Dr. King gave voice to, and my dad's fear of the Civil Rights Leader coming to Grosse Pointe both found an echo in my adolescent soul. I was conflicted.

The next time I made the trip to the Park branch of the Grosse Pointe Public Library with my class, I checked out a book about Dr. King. The title was, "Martin Luther King, Jr: The Peaceful Warrior."[184] I still had that book in my possession in April when, along with the rest of the students of GPCDS, I watched the funeral of Dr. King on a 19inch black-and-white television with rabbit ears. I wept during the televised funeral.

Five months before Dr. King's funeral, in November 1967, the Grosse Pointe Human Relations Council decided to invite a big-name Civil Rights speaker to the community. Several names were mentioned, and the first invitation went out by telephone to Roy Wilkins, Executive Secretary of the National Association for the Advancement of Colored People (NAACP). The call never reached Wilkins. He was already traveling with the Kerner Commission as they were putting together the report requested by President Johnson following the Detroit rebellion. The head of the planning committee for the Human Relations Council, Jude Huetteman, had a contact with the Southern Christian Leadership Conference (SCLC) who suggested she write Dr. King a letter and invite him. The contact promised to also write Dr. King a letter in support of the request. The response came on December 8: on Thursday, March 14, 1968, Dr. King would come to Grosse Pointe. The title of his speech: "The Future of Integration."

The next task was to find a large enough venue to hold the expected crowd. The Grosse Pointe High School auditorium was chosen, and a letter was sent to the Board requesting permission to use the facility. Normally such a letter from a community group would be rubber stamped, but it took the board two meetings to finally give its consent. The one condition was that the Human Rights Council purchase a one-million-dollar insurance policy to cover any damages that might occur.

Once the venue was secured, the committee faced the challenge of insuring adequate security for the event. One day, Huetteman received a phone call from the Chief of Police of Grosse Pointe Farms, Jack Roh, asking her to meet with him and other city officials to discuss the event.

At the meeting she learned that riot control plans were being drafted. The fear was that Black militants would use the opportunity to demonstrate. It soon became apparent that it was not Black militants but right-winged White activists who would be demonstrating. The FBI learned that these activists had forged some admission tickets to the event, and so would be inside the auditorium. Jack Roh knew there would be trouble and was preparing for any and every contingency.

Huetteman began noticing that her mail had been opened prior to her receiving it. She became suspicious that her phone was being tapped. Then one afternoon she received a phone call. "You think your kids are in school, don't you? Well, we've got them!" She immediately got into her car and made the four-minute drive to the school, where she gathered her children, who were safe, and returned to her home.[185]

A week before the event, the Grosse Pointe Property Owners Association, the same group that was responsible for the "point system" in use ten years earlier, sent a mass mailing to all the residents of the Pointes. The letter began: "In response to numerous inquiries directed to our office regarding the facts and circumstances of the scheduled appearance of the Reverend Martin Luther King, Jr. at the Grosse Pointe High School on March 14, 1968, we are giving you the following information." It went on, listing the names of the members of the Human Rights Council, the names and phone numbers of the School Board members noting how they voted, and the names of the three School Board members who were also members of the Human Rights Council: Alice Mary Hykes, Edward Pongracz, and Russell Peebles. On the reverse side of the mailing was an article by Frank S. Meyer, published in the January 16, 1968 issue of *National Review*. In the article Meyer writes: "For deliberation, adjustment, and justice . . . Dr.

King would substitute the assemblage of a militant mob, the provocation of violence, the stirring up of mass emotion, culminating in the *forcing* of his ideological prescriptions upon the constituted representatives of the republic. It is a program for government by force and the threat of force." While Dr. King had maintained his insistence on non-violence, the article made a direct connection with the developing radical wing of the Civil Rights movement and the followers of Malcolm X, connecting King with both Stokley Carmichael (who coined the term "Black Power") and H. Rap Brown (whose rhetoric included such incendiary phrases as "violence is as American as cherry pie" and that "If America don't come around, we're gonna burn it down."). "Preservation of civil order and firm defense of constitutional procedures against the revolutionary methods of Negro leaders like King, Carmichael and Brown," according to Meyers, "are measures necessary to the preservation of a free society in the United States; at the same time they are the indispensable prerequisites for any possible future advance of the Negro people."[186]

A second group, that went by the name the name "Breakthrough," also heard about Dr. King's upcoming visit to Grosse Pointe. Breakthrough was an anti-Communist group with White Supremacy tendencies.[187]  It was led by a Korean War veteran named Donald Lobsinger. In a later interview, Lobsinger said, "The 1960s were a communist- revolution that overturned most of the values in this country. It definitely was a revolution that took place in the 1960s. It turned this country upside down." He considered the riots that took place in Detroit and other cities during the summers "as dry runs for the big push that would result in the takeover of the United States by the communists."[188]

Lobsinger and the members of Breakthrough began developing plans for their response.  A flier was sent to members with the heading in all

caps: A CALL TO ACTION TO ALL BREAKTHROUGH MEMBERS
AND SUPPORTERS. The flier announced a "MEETING AND PEP
RALLY" to be held at the American Legion on Harper Avenue on
Detroit's east side on Tuesday prior to Dr. King's speech, and a
"DEMONSTRATION AGAINST MARTIN LUTHER KING, JR" to be
held during the speech on the schoolyard of Grosse Pointe High School.
The flyer continued:

> On Thursday, March 14th, MARTIN LUTHER KING, JR is
> scheduled to speak at the Grosse Pointe High School in Grosse
> Pointe. With your help we hope to give Mr. King the kind of
> reception he deserves in the form of the most spirited, largest and
> most impressive demonstration this city has seen yet.
> But we need YOUR help and cooperation (1) in recruiting
> persons for the demonstration, (2) distributing the enclosed leaflet,
> (3) painting signs and (4) in making sure you are at the
> demonstration YOURSELF. Let's show the NATION that WE
> MEAN BUSINESS. There will be a MEETING and PEP RALLY
> for Breakthrough members and supporters only to help instill the
> proper mood for the Demonstration two nights prior on Tuesday,
> March 12th. (see above). (For those who can afford only one night
> during the week—the Demonstration has priority).

The flyer went on to inform the members of three opportunities to
pick up leaflets to be distributed, including at the upcoming Sunday's
church services. Opportunities were listed to join in the painting of signs
for the demonstration. The flier summarized the members response
with a:

> REMINDER—An American—George Wallace—was not
> allowed to come into our city to speak. Halls are increasingly hard
> to find for our own meetings, and they have been cancelled in
> violation of signed contracts. Yet the Groppis, the King's, and the
> Carmicael's can come in here at their own leisure and preach their

hate and treason with impunity. But NO MORE! we say – NO MORE!

The flyer concluded with one final direction to the members: "Bring a large American Flag to the Demonstration." None of the addresses listed in the flyer were located in Grosse Pointe; they were all in Detroit. [189]

George Wallace, the "American" mentioned in the Breakthrough flier, was the governor of Alabama (mentioned in King's "I Have a Dream" speech) and a third-party Presidential Candidate in 1968. Seven months later and just days before the election, Wallace was allowed to speak in Detroit, holding a campaign rally at Cobo Hall downtown on October 29, 1968. While the majority of the crowd was pro-Wallace, a large number of anti-Wallace demonstrators were also present. When fighting began between the two groups, more than 350 police officers with nightsticks tried to disburse the crowd of 800 protesters, who fought back by throwing stones and other debris at the officers. The evening was another community-relations nightmare for the DPD, which was accused of numerous acts of excessive violence.[190]

On Monday, March 11, three days before Dr. King was scheduled to speak and the night before the Breakthrough Pep Rally, the Grosse Pointe Board of Education trustees held their monthly meeting. A standing-room-only crowd of residents gathered. The defeat of a recent millage vote was one of the concerns on the crowd's mind, but the major issue of concern was the upcoming visit of Dr. King. When the issue came up, one trustee, Arnold Fuchs, made a motion for the board to rescind the permit allowing Dr. King to speak. The motion failed by a vote of 5-2, the Board members voting the same way they initially did when they approved the permit. Questions were raised about the promised insurance policy the Human Rights Council was to purchase. The policy purchased by the Council included liability but not property coverage. According to Ray Arthur, director of business and finance for the board, such a policy was not available. The Human Rights Council had agreed to pay the $500 deductible on the school system's policy if there was any damage. Mr. Fuchs then questioned what school activities would be affected by this decision. The answer was that one adult-education class would be cancelled, at the request of the students. A final question was then raised about who would pay the cost of the extra police protection. A letter from Andrew Bremer, City Manager of Grosse Pointe Farms, suggested the School Board should be responsible for the cost of this extra protection. The Human Rights Council agreed to foot this cost as well.[191]

By the end of the discussion two things were clear: Dr. King would speak at the Grosse Pointe High School as scheduled, and there would likely be trouble. The trouble would not come from Black militants as my Dad and Chief Roh originally feared; the trouble would come from the White Supremacists. Not from the followers of Stokley Carmichael and H. Rap Brown, but from Breakthrough.

Dr. King was going through his own personal and spiritual struggle as Grosse Pointe was preparing for his visit. Ten months earlier Dr. King had given a speech at the Riverside Church in New York City where he spoke passionately against the Vietnam War. "I cannot forget that the Nobel Peace Prize was also a commission," he said,

> ...a commission to work harder than I had ever worked before for 'the brotherhood of man.' This is a calling that takes me beyond national allegiances, but even if it were not present, I would yet have to live with the meaning of my commitment to the ministry of Jesus Christ. To me the relationship of this ministry to the making of peace

is so obvious that I sometimes marvel at those who ask me why I am speaking against the war. Could it be that they do not know the good news was meant for all men, for communist and capitalist, for their children and ours, for Black and for White, for revolutionary and conservative? Have they forgotten that my ministry is in obedience to the One who loved his enemies so fully that he died for them? What then can I say to the Vietcong or to Castro or to Mao as a faithful minister of this One? Can I threaten them with death, or must I not share with them my life?

He went on, detailing the Vietnamese experience, including both the French and Japanese colonization, and their own battle for "liberation" under the leadership of Ho Chi Minh.

Our government felt then that the Vietnamese people were not 'ready' for independence, and we again fell victim to the deadly western arrogance that has poisoned the international atmosphere for so long. With that tragic decision we rejected a revolutionary government seeking self-determination, and a government that had been established not by China, for whom the Vietnamese have no great love, but by clearly indigenous forces that included some communists. For the peasants this new government meant real land reform, one of the most important needs in their lives.

Dr. King then gave a history of the U.S. military involvement in Vietnam, "giving voice to the voiceless in Vietnam and to understand the arguments of those who are called enemy," while stating he was "as deeply concerned about our own troops there as anything else."

I am convinced that if we are to get on the right side of the world revolution, we as a nation must undergo a radical revolution of values. We must rapidly begin to shift from a 'thing-oriented' society to a 'person-oriented' society. When machines and computer, profit motives and property rights are considered more important than people, the giant triplets of racism, extreme materialism, and militarism are incapable of being conquered.[192]

Along with his Vietnam War protest, Dr. King was preparing for a Poor People's March in Washington, D.C. in April. This was to be his non-violent response to the violent methods of Malcolm X, Stokley Carmichael and H. Rap Brown and the violence of the rioting that was now occurring every summer in the nation's cities. King increasingly viewed the Black struggle as a part of the struggle poor people of all races and nationalities faced in America. The marchers would call for massive government spending (from the savings that could result from ending the Vietnam war) as part of an "economic bill of rights." Included in the bill would be guaranteed employment for all able-bodied workers, a guaranteed livable income for those who were unable to work, an end to housing discrimination, and the enforcement of laws insuring integrated education.[193]

At a much deeper and more personal level, Dr. King was also wrestling with his own mortality. On Sunday, February 4, six weeks before arriving in Grosse Pointe, Dr. King preached a sermon at Ebenezer Baptist Church in Atlanta. Based on Mark 10:35-44, the sermon was entitled "The Drum Major Instinct." King told his audience that like James and John in the story, we all have a "drum major instinct—a desire to be out front, a desire to lead the parade, a desire to be first. . . The great issue of life is to harness the drum major instinct." In a surprise twist, King went on to tell his audience that Jesus *encourages* the "drum major instinct."

> Yes, don't give up this instinct. It's a good instinct if you use it right. It's a good instinct if you don't distort it and pervert it. Don't give it up. Keep feeling the need for being important. Keep feeling the need for being first. But I want you to be first in love. I want you to be first in moral excellence. I want you to be first in generosity. That is what I want you to do.

Like any good Christian preacher, King went on to apply the text to Jesus' greatness.

> I know a man—and I just want to talk about him a minute, and maybe you will discover who I'm talking about as I go down the way because he was a great one. And he just went about serving. He was born in an obscure village, the child of a poor peasant woman. And then he grew up in still another obscure village, where he worked as a carpenter until he was thirty years old. . . He was only thirty-three when the tide of public opinion turned against him. They called him a rabble-rouser. They called him a troublemaker. They said he was an agitator. He practiced civil disobedience; he broke injunctions. And so he was turned over to his enemies and went through the mockery of a trial. And the irony of it all is that his friends turned him over to them. One of his closest friends denied him. Another of his friends turned him over to his enemies. . . When he was dead, he was buried in a borrowed tomb, through the pity of a friend. Nineteen centuries have come and gone and today he stands as the most influential figure that ever entered human history. All of the armies that ever marched, all the navies that ever sailed, all the parliaments that ever sat, and all the kings that ever reigned put together have not affected the life of man on this earth as much as that one solitary life.

Dr. King ended the sermon, uncharacteristically, by reflecting on his own "one solitary life."

> Every now and then I guess we all think realistically about that day when we will be victimized with what is life's final common denominator—that something that we call death. We all think about it. And every now and then I think about my own death and I think about my own funeral. And I don't think of it in a morbid sense. And every now and then I ask myself, "What is it that I would want said?" And I leave the word to you this morning.
>
> If any of you are around when I have to meet my day, I don't want a long funeral. And if you get somebody to deliver the eulogy, tell them not to talk too long. And every now and then I wonder what I want them to say. Tell them not to mention that I have a

Nobel Peace Prize—that isn't important. Tell them not to mention that I have three or four hundred other awards—that's not important. Tell them not to mention where I went to school.

I'd like somebody to mention that day that Martin Luther King, Jr., tried to give his life serving others.

I'd like for somebody to say that day that Martin Luther King, Jr., tried to love somebody.

I want you to say that day that I tried to be right on the war question.

I want you to be able to say that day that I did try to feed the hungry.

And I want you to be able to say that day that I did try in my life to clothe those who were naked.

I want you to say on that day that I did try in my life to visit those who were in prison.

I want you to say that I tried to love and serve humanity.

Yes, if you want to say that I was a drum major, say that I was a drum major for justice. Say that I was a drum major for peace. I was a drum major for righteousness. And all of the other shallow things will not matter. I won't have any money to leave behind. I won't have the fine and luxurious things of life to leave behind. But I just want to leave a committed life behind. And that's all I want to say. [194]

The immediate feedback from a number of his friends and sympathizers to the sermon was negative. They felt it was gloomy and self-serving. But two months later Dr. King lay dead, the victim of an assassins' bullet in Memphis.

Andrew Young, King's close friend, later commented on the sermon: "Dr. King's faith was draining because people inside the organization were running around the country spouting talk about violence. . . More damaging to Dr. King was the flak we were getting from friends. They kept telling him he was failing."[195] It was a spiritually drained, deeply reflective, and depressed Dr. King who would speak in Grosse Pointe.

The announced title of Dr. King's speech was "The Future of Integration." However, the speech Dr. King actually gave was entitled "The Other America," a speech he had given eleven months earlier at Stanford University. Why the change? Perhaps it was the publication of the Kerner Report on February 29. On the very first page the Commission gave its assessment: "This is our basic conclusion. Our nation is moving toward two societies, one Black, one White—separate and unequal." The responsibility for the riots, according to the report, lies with the White community. The riots were a response to White racism, both individual and institutional. According to the Commission, "White society is deeply implicated in the ghetto. White institutions created it, White institutions maintain it, and White society condones it." On March 14, Dr. King would journey from the one society to the other, seeking to help the residents of Detroit's nationally known White affluent suburb understand "The Other America."

Dr. King missed his plane to Detroit that evening, and so would arrive an hour late. Mrs. Huetteman and her husband met him at his downtown hotel. During the twenty-minute ride to the high school Mrs. Huetteman briefed King on recent events in the community. The speaker exuded a sense of calm and peace, a peace that he continued to display throughout that eventful evening. All traffic was stopped within four blocks of the school, but their car was waved through the blockade. Chief Roh joined them at the foot of the driveway, slipped into the front seat of the car, and literally sat on Dr. King's lap to protect him. He was determined that nothing would happen to the Civil Rights leader on his watch.

Dr. King entered the back door of the auditorium and was immediately ushered to the podium, where he is introduced to a crowd of

3000 people by the Rt. Reverend Richard S. Emrich, Episcopal Bishop of Michigan. The crowd rose to its feet. Following a 5-minute standing ovation, King he began his speech.

It is always a very rich and rewarding experience when I can take a brief break from the day-to-day demands of our struggle for freedom and human dignity and discuss the issues involved in that struggle with concerned people of good will all over our nation and all over the world, and I certainly want to express my deep personal appreciation to you for inviting me to occupy this significant platform.

The Civil Rights leader, pastor's son, sharecropper's grandson, who grew up under the Jim Crow laws of Georgia and his predominately White audience from Detroit's wealthiest suburb began the evening by expressing their mutual respect for each other.

"I want to discuss the race problem tonight and I want to discuss it very honestly," King continued. "I want to use as a title for my lecture tonight, "The Other America." And I use this title because there are literally two Americas. Every city in our country has this kind of dualism, this schizophrenia, split at so many parts, and so every city ends up being two cities rather than one. There are two Americas." King then described the two Americas. "One America is beautiful for situation," he said. "In this America, millions of people have the milk of prosperity and the honey of equality flowing before them." He was talking about Grosse Pointe.

But there is another America. This other America has a daily ugliness about it that transforms the buoyancy of hope into the fatigue of despair. In this other America, thousands and thousands of people, men in particular walk the streets in search for jobs that do not exist. In this other America, millions of people are forced to live in vermin-filled, distressing housing conditions. . .

Courtesy of the Grosse Pointe Public School System

King continued with a subtle yet graphic image of the difference between the Other Americans and his Grosse Pointe audience: ". . . where they do not have the privilege of having wall-to-wall carpeting, but all too often, they end up with wall-to-wall rats and roaches."

The economic problem is the biggest challenge for the members of the Other America.

> There are so many other people in the other America who can never make ends meet because their incomes are far too low if they have incomes, and their jobs are so devoid of quality. And so in this other America, unemployment is a reality and under-employment is a reality.

At this point King was interrupted by a woman shouting in the audience. "I'll just wait until our friend can have her say." The audience applauds.

"I'll just wait until things are restored," King manages to say, and then makes a joke at the woman's expense. "Everybody talks about law and order." The crowd once again applauds.

"Now before I was so rudely interrupted," King continued. The audience once again applauses. "And I might say that it was my understanding that we're going to have a question and answer period, and if anybody disagrees with me, you will have the privilege, the opportunity to raise a question if you think I'm a traitor, then you'll have an opportunity to ask me about my traitorness and we will give you that opportunity."

"Now let me get back to the point that I was trying to bring out about the economic problem," King continued. "All too often when there is mass unemployment in the Black community, it's referred to as a social problem and when there is mass unemployment in the White community, it's referred to as a depression. But there is no basic difference." These words were not a part of the Stanford speech.

The audience gathered that evening, eight months after the Detroit rebellion, was obviously interested in King's views on the summer rioting occurring every year. The Civil Rights leader understood their concern and so expanded on his Stanford speech:

> Now I wanted to say something about the fact that we have lived over these last two or three summers with agony and we have seen our cities going up in flames. And I would be the first to say that I am still committed to militant, powerful, massive, non-violence as the most potent weapon in grappling with the problem from a direct-action point of view. I'm absolutely convinced that a riot merely intensifies the fears of the White community while relieving the guilt. And I feel that we must always work with an effective, powerful weapon and method that brings about tangible results. But it is not enough for me to stand before you tonight and condemn riots. It would be morally irresponsible for me to do that without, at the same time, condemning the contingent, intolerable conditions that exist in our society. These conditions are the things that cause individuals to feel that they have no other alternative than to engage in violent rebellions to get attention. And I must say tonight that a riot is the language of the unheard.

"The question," according to King, "is whether America is prepared to do something massively, affirmatively and forthrightly about the great problem we face in the area of race and the problem which can bring the curtain of doom down on American civilization if it is not solved." The first thing that needs to be done is that "there must be a recognition on the part of everybody in this nation that America is still a racist country." These words were not found in the Stanford speech, but clearly show the influence of the Kerner Report.

> However unpleasant that sounds, it is the truth. And we will never solve the problem of racism until there is a recognition of the fact that racism still stands at the center of so much of our nation and we must see racism for what it is. It is the nymph of an inferior people. It is the notion that one group has all of the knowledge, all of the insights, all of the purity, all of the work, all of the dignity. And another group is worthless, on a lower level of humanity, inferior. To

186

put it in philosophical language, racism is not based on some empirical generalization which, after some studies, would come to conclusion that these people are behind because of environmental conditions. Racism is based on an ontological affirmation. It is the notion that the very being of a people is inferior. And their ultimate logic of racism is genocide. Hitler was a very sick man. He was one of the great tragedies of history. But he was very honest. He took his racism to its logical conclusion. The minute his racism caused him to sickly feel and go about saying that there was something innately inferior about the Jew he ended up killing six million Jews. The ultimate logic of racism is genocide, and if one says that one is not good enough to have a job that is a solid quality job, if one is not good enough to have access to public accommodations, if one is not good enough to have the right to vote, if one is not good enough to live next door to him, if one is not good enough to marry his daughter because of his race. Then at that moment that person is saying that that person who is not good enough to do all of this is not fit to exist or to live. And that is the ultimate logic of racism. And we've got to see that this still exists in American society. And until it is removed, there will be people walking the streets alive and living in their humble dwellings feeling that they are nobody, feeling that they have no dignity and feeling that they are not respected. The first thing that must be on the agenda of our nation is to get rid of racism.

The second thing that needs to be done to combat racism, according to King, is to "get rid of two or three myths that still pervade our nation." Here King follows his Stanford speech quite closely. "One is the myth of time. . . the notion that only time can solve the problem of racial injustice." The second myth is "the notion that legislation can't solve the problem that you've got to change the heart." As a Baptist preacher, King observes that he is in the "heart changing business."

We are not going to have the kind of society that we should have until the White person treats the negro right - not because the law says it but because it's natural because it's right and because the Black man is the White man's brother. I'll be the first to say that we will never have a truly integrated society, a truly colorless society until men and women are obedient to the unenforceable.

But, King went on,

It may be true that morality cannot be legislated, but behavior can be regulated. It may be true that the law cannot change the heart but it can restrain the heartless. It may be true that the law can't make a man love me, but it can restrain him from lynching me, and I think that's pretty important also. And so while legislation may not change the hearts of men, it does change the habits of men when it's vigorously enforced and when you change the habits of people pretty soon attitudes begin to be changed and people begin to see that they can do things that fears caused them to feel that they could never do.

At this point Dr. King clearly lost his focus. The records of the speech do not include an interruption by hecklers. Perhaps there was some kind of commotion in the audience? Dr. King makes a joke about it: "I've been trying to think about what I'm going to preach about tomorrow down to Central Methodist Church in the Lenten series and I think I'll use as the text, 'Father forgive them for they know not what they do.'"

He then goes on, and gives a third myth, "and that is over-reliance on the bootstrap philosophy." While self-help is important, there is another side.

The other day I was on a plane and a man started talking with me and he said I'm sympathetic toward what you're trying to do, but I just feel that you people don't do enough for yourself and then he went on to say that my problem is, my concern is, that I know of other ethnic groups, many of the ethnic groups that came to this country and they had problems just as negroes and yet they did the job for themselves, they lifted themselves by their own bootstraps. Why is it that negroes can't do that?

Dr. King responds that no other ethnic group was enslaved in this country. Further, King says, "America made the Black man's color a stigma." Black is something that is equated with evil in our language.

If you open Roget's Thesaurus and notice the synonym for Black, you'll find about a hundred and twenty and most of them represent something dirty, smut, degrading, low, and when you turn to the synonym for White, about one hundred and thirty, all of them represent something high, pure, chaste. You go right down that list. And so in the language a White life is a little better than a Black life. Just follow. If somebody goes wrong in the family, we don't call him a White sheep we call him a Black sheep. And then if you block somebody from getting somewhere you don't say they've been White balled, you say they've been Blackballed. And just go down the line. It's not Whitemail it's Blackmail. I tell you this to seriously say that the nation made the Black man's color a stigma.

Dr, King is coming close to the end of his speech, but before he sits down there are two other things he wants to say. The first was regarding the Vietnam War.

I want to say that if we're to move ahead and solve this problem we must re-order our national priorities. Today we're spending almost thirty-five billion dollars a year to fight what I consider an unjust, ill-considered, evil, costly, unwinnable war at Viet Nam. I wish I had time to go into the dimensions of this. But I must say that the war in Viet Nam is playing havoc with our domestic destinies. That war has torn up the Geneva accord, it has strengthened, it has substituted . . .

Once again Dr. King is interrupted, this time by a Navy Petty Officer, who is particularly boisterous and accuses King of treason.[196] The Civil Rights speaker shows the young man absolute respect and invites him to the podium.

"Ladies and gentlemen," the young man says, "my name is Joseph McLawtern, communications technician, U.S. Navy, United States of America and I fought for freedom. I didn't fight for Communism, traitors, and I didn't fight to be sold down the drain. Not by Romney, Cavanagh, Johnson - nobody, nobody's going to sell me down the drain."

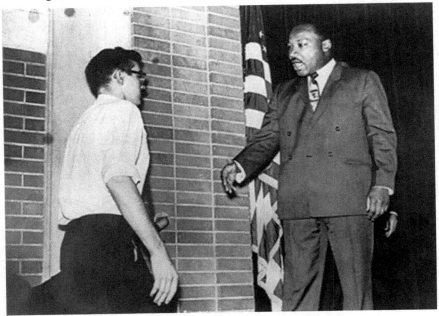

Courtesy of the Grosse Pointe Public School System

"Alright, thank you very much." King responds, "I just want to say in response to that, that there are those of us who oppose the war in Viet Nam. I feel like opposing it for many reasons. Many of them are moral reasons but one basic reason is that we love our boys who are fighting there and we just want them to come back home."

The war was an unjust war according to King, and risks bringing the world to nuclear annihilation. "I think it would be rather absurd for me to work for integrated schools and not be concerned about the survival of the world in which to integrate." The issue is an issue of justice. "For me justice is indivisible. Injustice anywhere is a threat to justice everywhere." The war is harming the cause of civil rights. "I think the war in Viet Nam hurt civil rights much more than my taking a stand against the war." King has no choice but to take a stand against the war—that is the kind of leader he was.

Ultimately, a genuine leader is not a succor for consensus but a mold of consensus. And on some positions, cowardice asks the question is it safe? Expediency asks the question is it politics? Vanity asks the question is it popular? The conscience asks the question is it right? And there comes a time when one must take a position that is neither safe nor politics nor popular but he must do it because conscience tells him it is right.

Returning to the issue of riots and a positive response to them, King continues. "I've been searching for a long time for an alternative to riots on the one hand and timid supplication for justice on the other and I think that alternative is found in militant, massive non-violence." This was how the movement made a difference before, when President Johnson said he couldn't get a voting rights bill passed. A massive gathering in Selma, Alabama, made the difference. So will the upcoming gathering in Washington.

The final thing King said before taking his seat was in the realm of the spirit.

In the midst of the hollering and in the midst of the discourtesy tonight, we got to come to see that however much we dislike it, the destinies of White and Black America are tied together... Somehow, we must all learn to live together as brothers in this country or we're all going to perish together as fools. Our destinies are tied together. Whether we like it or not culturally and otherwise, every White person is a little bit negro and every negro is a little bit White. Our language, our music, our material prosperity and even our food are an amalgam of Black and White, so there can be no separate Black path to power and fulfillment that does not intersect White routes and there can ultimately be no separate White path to power and fulfillment short of social disaster without recognizing the necessity of sharing that power with Black aspirations for freedom and human dignity. We must come to see. . .yes we do need each other, the Black man needs the White man to save him from his fear and the White man needs the Black man to free him from his guilt.

Following a reference to John Donne's meditation, "No Man is an Island," the Baptist preacher inside King's soul reveals himself as the speaker sums up his message. "We are going to win our freedom because both the sacred heritage of our nation and the eternal will of the Almighty God are embodied in our echoing demands." The Black preacher then concludes in classic style, insisting the old spiritual is correct: "We Shall Overcome."

"We shall overcome because Carlisle is right. "No lie can live forever." We shall overcome because William Cullen Bryant is right. "Truth crushed to earth will rise again." We shall overcome because James Russell Lowell is right. "Truth forever on the scaffold, wrong forever on the throne." Yet that scaffold sways the future. We shall overcome because the Bible is right. "You shall reap what you sow." With this faith we will be able to hew out of the mountain of despair, a stone of hope. With this faith we will be able to transform the jangling discords of our nation into a beautiful symphony of brotherhood. With this faith we will be able to speed up the day when all of God's children all over this nation - Black men and White men, Jews and Gentiles, Protestants and Catholics will be able to join hands and sing in the words of the old negro spiritual, 'Free at Last, Free at Last, Thank God Almighty, We are Free At Last.'"[197]

Following the speech, King held a press conference where he commented that he had never experienced such vocal opposition at an indoor meeting. He was visibly shaken.[198] This only reinforced the negative image Grosse Pointe had when it came to race relations. One of King's biographers wrote: "On March 17, he [King] interrupted a Southern recruitment drive for the [Poor People's] campaign to speak in the barony of Detroit's wealthy, Grosse Pointe. He was outrageously heckled for his Vietnam views,"[199] and later refers to his "unsettling reception in Grosse Pointe, Michigan."[200] These are certainly both true statements, but what they overlook the fact that the crowd that night, mostly Grosse Pointers, welcomed Dr. King enthusiastically. Those who so rudely interrupted the speaker that night were overwhelmingly from outside the Pointes. This is similar to what happened when Dr. Gordon Wright moved into Grosse Pointe Woods. Although there was strong opposition to him moving into the community from some Grosse Pointers, their voices were magnified by others who did not live in the Pointes. Vocal racists from across the city seemed to be attracted to Grosse Pointe.

There were at least three members of The Fort in the audience the night Dr. King came to Grosse Pointe. Mariam Schaafsma was a teacher in the Detroit Public School system. She eventually completed a twenty-year career in the system teaching kindergarten children composed almost exclusively of African American children. Mariam was accompanied by her daughter Mary Helen, a student at Grosse Pointe High School. Mary Helen was one of the students at Grosse Pointe High School that signed the open letter to teachers encouraging them to consider teaching in Grosse Pointe, no matter what their background, race, or religion. She went on to be a social worker in Chicago and a passionate advocate for social justice.

The third member of The Fort in attendance that evening was the pastor, Reverend Frank Steen.

From The Fort, located in the shadow of Altar and Mack, both Americas were visible. Grosse Pointe was the America where "people have the milk of prosperity and the honey of equality flowing before them." But "The Other America," the America with "a daily ugliness about it that transforms the buoyancy of hope into the fatigue of despair." was just a few miles to the west. Dr. Steen's preaching began to show the influence of Dr. King's speech. He started challenging the members of The Fort to look at "The Other America." He didn't use Dr. King's exact words, but the message was the same. "The next time you drive downtown," he would say from the pulpit, "Don't take the expressway. Take the surface streets. Look around you. Ask yourselves what the church's responsibility is in all this." People of Grosse Pointe, members of The Fort: open your eyes to "the other America."

As might be expected, it was also a question that was met with fear and resistance. The bell-bottom pants wearing pastor who made reference to *All in the Family* was now hitting close to home. The members of The Fort were challenged to move beyond a faith that was simply about individual salvation and personal holiness to a concern for the good of society around them—what later became known as Social Justice. The Fort was moving into uncharted territory, where the old walls of tradition and separation from others would no longer provide security and protection. The Fort was changing from a Dutch church to a Detroit church.

Frank Steen's ministry and the question about the church's responsibility toward the community in which it was placed made a huge impression on me and continued to burn in my soul as I moved on to college, seminary, and throughout my life.

*"It takes a tough mind and a tender heart to hold on to hope."*
-Dr. Raphael Warnock[201]

*Are we tough enough to build a church that forces kids like me to engage with the world rather than withdraw from it?*
-J.D. Vance[202]

*"Detroit has ruined me for living anywhere else and I won't be able to take back the ideas that have grown from what I've seen."*
-Drew Philip[203]

# Epilogue

# Legacy

The Fort still stands today, in the shadow of Alter and Mack. It continues to tower over Grosse Pointe Park's humble cabbage patch neighborhood, the same massive Calvinistic Cathedral it has always been. The woodwork, including the pews, pulpit and chancel are the same dark walnut. The walls have been painted a much lighter color, which brightens the entire sanctuary. Sermons based on the Bible are still preached, the congregation still divided into three sections by the two aisles. The organ continues to be the main instrument used to accompany congregational singing, although the words are now projected on a screen behind the pulpit.

The Fort is still affiliated with the Christian Reformed Church. But it is no longer a Dutch Church. Many young families representing a wide variety of ethnic backgrounds have chosen to purchase homes in the Cabbage Patch neighborhood, especially since the 2008 housing crash. Some of these new families have chosen to affiliate with The Fort because that is the neighborhood church. Children today nearly outnumber adults on Sunday morning.

The parking lot problem has been solved. A house next to the parking lot, owned by the church and used to house Christian School teachers, has been torn down to make room for additional parking. The addition of landscaping at the parking lot's entrance enhances the beauty of the entire complex.

The Grosse Pointe Christian Day School did not fare as well. An aging congregation in the early 2000s and the development of Charter Schools took their toll. The school closed its doors in 2004. The student body at that time was predominately African American.

The church has begun a new outreach ministry, a preschool that operates under the name of "God's Kids," and uses the space formerly occupied by the Christian School. If you were to stop in at The Fort on any weekday you would see a United Nations gathering of children—White, African American, Asian, and Hispanic. Some of the families of these children can be seen in church on Sunday morning.

Grosse Pointe continues to be a desirable community. The yards are still immaculately manicured, the five communities still served by their own police and fire departments and the five exclusive lakefront parks. All five Grosse Pointes have African American residents. Grosse Pointe Park, the community where The Fort is located, has the highest percentage of African American residents of all the Grosse Pointes with 8.4%.[204]

Detroit has changed significantly since the 1960s. White flight to the suburbs following the riots, the scourge of drugs, mismanagement in municipal government, and the 2013 bankruptcy have all taken their toll. In 1975 the congregation of The Fort considered a proposal to move to Macomb County. The members chose to continue to be a part of the neighborhoods surrounding Mack and Alter. Today the Detroit neighborhoods on the other side of either Altar or Mack from Grosse Pointe Park are mostly fields composed of empty lots and streets desperately in need of repair. The majority of the homes were burned either as a result of squatters doing drugs or the infamous Devil's Night tradition.[205]

The members of The Fort continue to be concerned about the social issues of their surrounding community. In recent years, their concern has focused on the issue of housing. Two blocks north on Maryland Avenue, just across Mack, the vacant lots so prevalent in the city emerge. But five blocks further a neighborhood of brand new, 1500 square foot homes with aluminum siding and attached two stall garages proudly rises up out of the fields of vacant lots. The Fort continues to work with the other churches in Grosse Pointe, and the members of this spiritual coalition have partnered with Habitat for Humanity to erect an entire neighborhood in Detroit. In many ways this new neighborhood in Detroit is more attractive than the Cabbage Patch surrounding The Fort. The members of The Fort and the Christian Reformed denomination of which they are a part continue to be concerned for the spiritual needs of their neighbors, and so they are starting a new church—a "house church" for the residents of this new community. It will be a church focused on both the spiritual and physical needs of its members and the surrounding community.

I left Grosse Pointe, Detroit, and The Fort in 1974, taking the experiences of eight years in the Motor City with me. They have formed me. The Fort, tucked away in the shadow of Mack and Altar, and the Christian School attached to it has molded and shaped my life in ways that have taken years for me to fully appreciate. The words of Drew Philip, written 43 years later, were true for me. "Detroit has ruined me for living anywhere else and I won't be able to take back the ideas that have grown from what I've seen." I knew privilege as a White kid from Grosse Pointe. But I had also been exposed to "The Other America." I knew the America where, in Dr. King's words, "millions of people have the milk of prosperity and the honey of equality flowing before them." I had also seen the America that had "a daily ugliness about it that transforms the buoyancy of hope into the fatigue of despair." I knew that Dr. King's words were true for Detroit and Grosse Pointe, that there was "this kind of dualism, this schizophrenia, split at so many parts, and so every city ends up being two cities rather than one." I knew about injustice, not as a victim, but as an observer. I had heard "the language of the unheard" in the 1967 riot. "And what is it America has failed to hear?" Dr. King asked. "It has failed to hear that the plight of the Negro poor has worsened over the last twelve or fifteen years. It has failed to hear that the promises of freedom and justice have not been met. And it has failed to hear that large segments of White society are more concerned about tranquility and the status quo than about justice and humanity."

Frank Steen, the pastor of The Fort, made sure that I not only heard the voices of the Negro poor but also saw their suffering. "Next time you go downtown, don't take the expressway. Take the surface streets. Look around you and ask yourselves what the church's responsibility is in all this." The ride from Grosse Pointe to downtown Detroit is a very different trip depending on whether you choose to take the Edsel Ford Freeway or a surface street like Charlevoix or Kerchival. The surface streets allow the driver to see the neighborhoods, to see the people. Homeless people gathered at the corners asking for handouts from those waiting for the traffic light to turn green. Men unable to find work sitting on their front porches smoking cigarettes. Elderly women waiting for the few busses that serve the city, bundled up in their heavy coats to keep out the cold. Young men loitering on street corners; young women dressed in provocative clothing. A drunk sleeping in a doorway. These are the images of poverty, on full display from the surface streets. I had seen all of this.

Those who take the freeway don't need to view this suffering and poverty. Most of the freeways of Detroit are below grade. Some of them are lined with walls. These walls hide the suffering of the urban neighborhoods from the eyes of suburban travelers. Walls are an effective way to ease the discomfort that comes from seeing the plight of the suffering and the injustice that produces that suffering. Since I left in 1974, Grosse Pointe has constructed several barriers, physical walls at the end of streets that formerly opened out to Alter or Mack. These walls effectively turn the streets of Grosse Pointe into col-du-sacs at the city limits. They are physical barriers between the people of the Pointes and Detroit. They help maintain the distinctions between the two Americas. The city "ends up being two cities rather than one." [206]

On that Sunday morning in February 1966 when my family and I first attended the morning service at The Fort, we found a church that in many ways saw itself as a fort, gathered safely behind a different kind of walls. These walls were built from ethnic traditions and rigid doctrinal distinctions, and effectively kept out those who might differ from the members of the church. The history of The Fort is the story of the journey of one spiritual community from building walls to tearing them down.

Some walls, of course, need to stay. Walls help define a community. They give voice to values and principles under which the members of a community live. The walls of the Christian tradition led the pastors and key laymen and women of Grosse Pointe to disavow racism and to fight for open housing. The walls of the Reformed faith required the Board of the Grosse Pointe Christian Day School to admit African-American students because they were defined first of all not by their race but by the fact that they were a part of the Christian community.

The question is, which walls need to be reinforced and which walls need to be torn down?

In its own quiet way, The Fort has had an influence far beyond her own membership, the communities of Detroit and Grosse Pointe, or the Christian Reformed Church. The two young men identified in Chapter Four both grew up to be ministers in the Christian Reformed denomination. Jacob Eppinga, who spent his free time in evangelistic work served a large downtown church, LaGrave Avenue Christian Reformed Church. This influential congregation is located in the city where the denomination maintained its headquarters, Grand Rapids, MI. For years Eppinga wrote a weekly column in the denomination's magazine, *The Banner*, entitled "Of Cabbages and Kings." The popular column generally had a one-word title, which Eppinga would reflect on and eventually draw a Biblical lesson. Lewis Smedes, who was attracted to the "fleshpots of Egypt" found in the Burlesque shows downtown, eventually taught ethics at Fuller Theological Seminary and authored sixteen books, including popular titles such as *Sex for Christians,  Forgive and Forget: Healing the Hurts We Don't Deserve,* and

Reverend Jacob Eppinga. Photo courtesy of Heritage Hall, the archives of the Christian Reformed Church located at Calvin University and Calvin Theological Seminary, Grand Rapids, MI.

*Shame and Grace: Healing the Shame We Don't Deserve."* Another

young man from the congregation, Duane VanderBrug, worked for years in the denomination's Home Missions office, focusing on planting churches in minority communities. Two laymen from the congregation, Dr. Philip Feringa (the Christian School Board president) and Judge Feikens both served on the original Synodical Committee on Race Relations (SCORR), a standing committee established by Synod to assist the denomination to address issues of racial prejudice within her membership in response to the conflict between the Lawndale Church and Timothy Christian School in Cicero, IL.

The influence of The Fort and the Grosse Pointe Christian Day

Reverend Lewis Smedes. Photo courtesy of Heritage Hall, the archives of the Christian Reformed Church, Calvin University, and Calvin Theological Seminary, Grand Rapids, MI.

School can also be seen in the life of Jarrett Bell, the young man from the Community Church who shoveled the snow from Rosa Parks' sidewalk. Jarrett began attending the Christian School in Grosse Pointe beginning in the autumn of 1969, one year after the school was first integrated. Jarrett was a bright young man. Before enrolling in the Grosse Pointe school, he had been double promoted to the fourth grade in his Detroit school. The question was raised, would the Christian School recognize the double promotion from the Detroit school? He was given a placement test and was placed in the fourth grade. "Everything looks good," he was told. "but we need to work on your reading comprehension."

The third and fourth grade teacher that year was Helen Ottenhoff, who was dating a young man named Paul Van Wyke. Paul would regularly visit his girlfriend's classroom, and the two of them took a special interest in Jarrett. As Jarrett tells the story, he met Paul "jiving about this and that," and soon Paul became a Big Brother to Jarrett. For five years Paul served in that role, taking Jarrett to his family's

Reverend Duane Vanderbrug. Photo courtesy of Heritage Hall, the archives of the Christian Reformed Church, Calvin University, and Calvin Theological Seminary, Grand Rapids, MI.

summer home in Illinois on multiple occasions. Meanwhile, Helen noticed Jarrett's passion for sports, and encouraged it. He was asked on one occasion to give a sports report to the class. The other kids thought he was the "teacher's pet," which he may well have been. After Paul and Helen were married and Jarrett was no longer her student, he would spend weekends at their home in the teacher's flat next door to The Fort. Jarrett's life was enriched by his time at the school and with the Van Wyke's. His background in Virginia Park made him worldlier than others his age, while his experiences in Grosse Pointe gave him a positive view on life. He values the dual cultural experience of living in Virginia Park and receiving a Christian education in Grosse Pointe.

The time came when Jarrett graduated from Grosse Pointe Christian School and had to return to the Detroit Public School system. He enrolled at Northwestern, the same school where the students had walked out of class eight years earlier. During his first year he got all "A's," in large measure because his older sister was also there and helped him through the experience. But like William Scott in Chapter Two, the transition back to the world of Virginia Park was difficult. The cultural shock was overwhelming. He had no social network and had to make new friends. He found the regular fights on the schoolyard to be intimidating.

Jarrett started skipping school, which turned out to be his downfall. He learned later that after 18 unexcused absences a student received an automatic "F" for the course. Jarrett ended up flunking the 10th grade. Rather than attending school, Jarrett would spend time at Olympia stadium with Detroit Red Wings. "It was the most fascinating place for me," he said. He found odd jobs around the stadium, working on projects for the PR Department of the Detroit Red Wings. The General Manager of the team, Alex Delvecchio, paid him out of his own pocket.

Jarrett made up the 10th grade and by taking summer school classes he was able to complete High School on time. From there he went to Michigan State University, where he graduated in 1981 with a degree in Communication.

Today Jarrett is an NFL Columnist for USA TODAY Sports based in Tysons Corner, Virginia and a practicing Christian. "If I didn't go to Grosse Pointe, who knows what would have happened?"[207]

Like Jarrett Bell, my transition out of The Fort was not an easy one. Like most young people from the church, I chose to attend the denominational college, Calvin College (now Calvin University) in Grand Rapids, Michigan. My goal was to move on to Calvin Seminary, located on the same campus as the College, and eventually become an ordained minister in the Christian Reformed denomination. My hope was that I could serve a congregation in a large city and serve both the White and the African American community. I naïvely believed that in the church people from different backgrounds could come together and the wounds on display in the July 1967 riots could begin to be healed. I still believe that.

At Calvin College I was told that, if I wanted to be a Christian Reformed minister, I first had to take Dutch. Calvin Seminary required a modern foreign language as well as a year of Latin and two years of Greek for admission. Dutch was the preferred modern language, but German would be an acceptable alternative.

"Why would I want to take Dutch?" I asked. "How would that make me a better minister in a place like Detroit?" I thought.

"You need to take Dutch so that you can read Dutch theologians in the original language," was the reply.

"Why would I want to do that?" I asked. "If it is really important, someone will translate it into English."

"You don't have any appreciation for your heritage," was the reply.

I did have an appreciation for my heritage. My heritage was American. As a fifth-generation American who had spent his developing years in Detroit, I had fully Americanized. The church I hoped to someday serve and the church's seminary were not yet there. I was looking for American answers to American questions, like the racism that still plagued the nation over a hundred years after Black slaves were set free. The seminary in many ways was a colonial institution, looking back to the motherland for direction.

So I took Dutch. I took Dutch with a class full of Canadians, children of post-World War II immigrants from the Netherlands whose parents spoke Dutch in the home. They got an easy "A." I struggled to pull off a "C" or a "D."

Four years later I enrolled in Calvin Seminary, Frank Steen's challenge still ringing in my ears. "Next time you go downtown, don't take the expressway. Take the surface streets. Look around you and ask yourselves what the church's responsibility is in all this." I found a faculty at the seminary that included some who were struggling with questions like this. Many of them lived in a predominately African American neighborhood near the Seminary's old campus in the inner city. Other faculty members could not even hear my question or didn't understand the emotion and passion behind it. I got no answers. Instead, I got answers to questions I was not asking. In Systematic Theology I read many of the works of a Dutch theologian, G.C. Berkouwer. I learned about a place called the Free University of Amsterdam, where a number of my classmates intended to go after seminary graduation to pursue graduate studies. I figured "Free University" meant no tuition, although that didn't seem possible. No one told me that it was free from Government control and the State run Dutch Reformed Church. I learned about Karl Barth, probably the most influential theologian of the twentieth century. My professor studied under Barth, but was constantly pointing out where he was wrong. I couldn't figure out why we were spending so much time on this man if he was wrong.

I was learning about walls. Ethnic and theological walls that kept the church safe. Anything outside the theological walls of Dutch theology was either ignored or met with a great deal of skepticism. I had my own need to feel safe, and to be accepted by this church that I hoped would eventually ordain me as a minister, so I conformed as much as I could. Conservative was safe. I was conservative. The big issue of the day was the ordination of women to the ministry. I was convinced that the Bible was clear on the matter, and quoted the texts that Conservatives used to end all discussion. I tried to believe what they told me to believe.

But I also wanted to learn how to minister in Detroit. No one pointed me to Reinhold Niebuhr, a theologian at Union Seminary in New York City who had served from 1915 to 1928 as pastor of the Bethel Evangelical Church, a congregation of German autoworkers in Detroit. Early in his time at Bethel, Niebuhr embraced the Social Gospel. But over time he became disillusioned with the movement. He was also a student of Karl Barth. These American—and Michigan—connections would have made theology so much more relevant. They could have been used to challenge my mind, to stimulate my thinking. But theology was presented in an academic way that seemed irrelevant to me. I was angry and confused.

My third year at Seminary, my wife and I moved to Chicago. Calvin Seminary, along with several other midwestern Seminaries, had developed a program entitled Seminary Consortium on Urban Pastoral Education (SCUPE), and I chose to participate in that program. In Chicago I discovered teachers who, like me, had a passion for the city. One of them, William "Bud" Ipema, was Christian Reformed. He taught our class, made up of students from several midwestern seminaries, about a Dutch Theologian named Abraham Kuyper. Kuyper was famous for his quote, "Every square inch of this world belongs to God." Ipema translated that into an urban context. "Every city block belongs to God." This was theology I could understand and relate to. As Christians our job is to reclaim those city blocks for the God who created the entire universe and is Lord over all. It was an inspiring vision, one too big to ever fulfill, but worth a lifetime of effort to try. I became a Kuyperian. I later learned that Kuyper was the man who founded the Free University of Amsterdam, and that he served as Prime Minister of the Netherlands.

After studying in Chicago for a year, I returned to Grand Rapids to complete my final year at Calvin Seminary. In April of that final year my faculty advisor called me into his office and informed me that the faculty was not going to recommend me for ordination. "You're not ready, not yet" he said. "The faculty feels you are too immature." I was certainly immature—I was only 24—but I also had the sense that I didn't fit the mold. I spent the following year back in Detroit, as a student at Harper Hospital in the Clinical Pastoral Education (CPE) program. The following April I was interviewed for an hour by a Calvin Seminary professor who was driving through the city on the way to Canada and was pronounced ready to be ordained. I tried to fit the mold. I served two rural Christian Reformed congregations. Eventually I became a Chaplain in the United States Navy, where I could work comfortably with people from all walks of life.

J.D. Vance asks the question: "Are we tough enough to build a church that forces kids like me to engage with the world rather than withdraw from it?" For a large number of Americans, this is an irrelevant question. They have chosen not to cultivate a faith-life. Many are atheists. Others have chosen to identify with a particular religion without identifying with an organized body that would help them in the practice of their faith. Such people will say, "I'm spiritual but not religious." The number of people who have left the Christian church since 1970 is staggering. A whole generation (or two) has grown up with no religious affiliation. When asked to check a box identifying their religious preference, they check the box marked "none." I have written this book with such people in mind and respect their choices.

But I have also told this story in part to challenge such people to take another look at the church.

Many would label the church today as narrow-minded, racist, homophobic, and with other labels. The evidence supporting such accusations is overwhelming. Many have been hurt by churches that were intolerant and unaccepting of people who didn't fit their mold. The incidents of young people being sexually abused while participating in church programs, whether as Roman Catholic altar boys or in Protestant Bible camps, is staggering. For this I grieve. The church has much to confess, and many whose forgiveness it needs to seek.

But that is not the whole story of the church. It has also been a formative force for good in the lives of millions of young people, including Jarrett Bell and myself. It has called society to follow a higher standard with its message of love for God and love for neighbor, a call that needs to be heard more today than ever before in a society that is materially rich but spiritually poor. The church has been one of the greatest advocates for the poor and disadvantaged. This is as true of many churches in America today as are the negative labels that are so often used. The truth, as is so often the case, is not "either or" but "both and." The church is both broken and sinful and an important institution without which society would be greatly impoverished.

For those who have not yet given up on the church, J.D. Vance's question poses a challenge. "Are we tough enough to build a church that forces kids like me to engage with the world rather than withdraw from it?" Are we tough enough to build a church that forces both White kids from privileged Grosse Pointe (like myself) and Black kids from our nation's inner cities (like Jarrett Bell) to engage with the world and offer moral, godly leadership wherever their life's journeys take them, whether that be the U.S. military or the sports department of a national newspaper?

Two words come to mind in answer to J. D. Vance's question—one secular, one religious, but both mean the same thing: mentoring and discipleship. This is what Helen and Paul Van Wyke did for Jarrett Bell. They mentored him. They discipled him. They showed him a different way of life. A way of that was different from the violent way he learned in Virginia Park and the self-centered material way on display in Grosse Pointe. In that humble flat, the Van Wykes showed him a way of life based on following the teachings of Jesus. A way of life where love for God and love for neighbor were central. A message not just preached from the pulpit but modeled in a living room.

The influence of the church in American society has declined drastically since the 1960s. That has been a loss for our society. The Mainline Churches of Grosse Pointe served as the moral conscience of the community in the fight for open housing. Since that time, the Mainline Churches have experienced huge membership losses. With this membership loss has come a loss of influence. The Evangelical Churches have not replaced the Mainline Churches as the moral conscience of society, with the exception of the issue of abortion. The gap has been filled by the legal profession. Far too often the deciding question in society is not, "is it right" (the moral question) but "is it legal?"

I believe the church is as important today as it ever was. Society needs tough churches that are not solely focused on the afterlife, but willing to engage with this world, with all the struggles, ambiguity, and suffering that such engagement entails.

We need churches like The Fort.

## Notes

---

1

From the documentary film, "American Revolution: The Evolution of Grace Lee Boggs."

2

John Howard Griffin, *Black Like Me.* (Cutchogue, New York: Buccaneer Books, 1960) 123.

3

Will Herberg, *Protestant, Catholic, Jew.* (Chicago: University of Chicago Press, 1955) 256.

4

*Grosse Pointe Historical Society*
http://www.gphistorical.org/mlk/mlkspeech/index.htm (accessed August 22, 2020).

5

Technically "The Great Trek" refers to the migration of the Dutch in South Africa north and eastward in response to the British colonization of the Cape Colony. The Dutch historian Jacob Van Hinte uses this term to refer to the 19th Century Dutch immigration to America in his seminal work, *Netherlanders in America: The Study of Emigration and Settlement in the 19th and 20th Centuries in the United States of America,* trans. by Adriaan de Wit. (Grand Rapids, MI: Baker Book House, 1985).

6

Adrian Van Koevering, *Legends of the Dutch* (Zeeland, MI: Zeeland Record Co, 1960) 211.

7

Ibid, 213.

8

"No person held to service or labor in one state, under the laws thereof, escaping into another, shall, in consequence of any law or regulation therein, be discharged from such service or labor, but shall be delivered up on claim of the party to whom such service or labor may be due."

Constitution of the United States of America, Article IV, section 2, clause 3. This was rendered moot by the passage of the 13th Amendment in 1865.

9

"That when a person held to labor in any of the United States, or in either of the Territories on the Northwest or South of the Ohio river, under the laws thereof, shall escape into any other part of the said States or Territory, the person to whom such labor or service may be due, his agent or attorney, is hereby empowered to seize or arrest such fugitive from labor, and to take him or her before any Judge of the Circuit or District Courts of the United States, residing or being within the State, or before any magistrate of a county, city, or town corporate, wherein such seizure or arrest shall be made, and upon proof to the satisfaction of such Judge or magistrate, either by oral testimony or affidavit taken before and certified by a magistrate of any such State or Territory, that the person so seized or arrested, doth, under the laws of the State or Territory from which he or she fled, owe service or labor to the person claiming him or her, it shall be the duty of such Judge or magistrate to give a certificate thereof to such claimant, his agent, or attorney, which shall be sufficient warrant for removing the said fugitive from labor to the State or Territory from which he or she fled." Fugitive Slave Act of 1793.

10

In 1917 there were 2,874 African Americans working in the 20 largest industrial firms in Detroit; by 1919 the number had skyrocketed to 11,000. B. J. Widick, *Detroit: City of Race and Class Violence.* (Detroit: Wayne State University Press, 1972), 26.

11

Compass directions are confusing here. The Detroit River actually flows east/west out of Lake St. Clair until it makes a turn in downtown Detroit, so Grosse Pointe is east, not north of Detroit. If you go directly south from Grosse Pointe Park, you will hit Canada. This is the only place where the United States is due north of Canada.

12

In 1990 the First Christian Reformed Church of Detroit was listed on the Michigan State Registration of Historic Places. In a letter dated January 3, 1990 to Reverend William DeVries, pastor of First Church at the time, Martha M. Bigelow, Director of the Bureau of History and Executive

Secretary of the Michigan Historical Commission wrote of the building: "The First Christian Reformed Church is a compound massed planned brick edifice presenting an irregular silhouette and revealing Collegiate Gothic stylistic affiliation. Its façade is composed of a central gabled and parapeted bay enclosing an outscaled tudor arched stained glass window. It is flanked by two towered entry bays, each supported at the corners by stepped buttresses with masonry coping. The southern tower bay is two stories tall and anchors pared entry doors enframed within a masonry tudor arch, rising to a crenelated parapet. The northern tower bay is similar but rises three stories to an enclosed belfry lacking a spire but exhibiting louvered tudor arched masonry surrounds above an enclosed cameo window. Masonry string courses define each story within the façade bays, and additional decoration is supplied by recessed panels and brick pilasters. The façade's central stained glass windowdesign is repeated in the gabled transcept of the north elevation, while a six sided hipped roof apse composes most of the ediface's south elevation. The interior of the church features covered plaster ceilings with wooden ribs and is lighted by the large tudor arched stained glass windows. The arches are repeated in the ceiling profile and also enframe the Chancel. Wainscoting occurs along all nave walls."

13

Smokey Robinson and Ronald White, *My Girl,* copyright Global Music Rights, 1965.

14

The Heidelberg Catechism is one of the three statements of faith that lay out the doctrinal beliefs of the Christian Reformed Church and other Reformed Churches around the world. It was written in the city of Heidelberg, Germany in 1563 and is made up of 129 Questions and Answers. Before the days of modern educational methods children would memorize the answers and their teachers would quiz them by asking the questions to which they would respond with the answers. Early on these 129 Questions and Answers were divided into 52 "Lord's Days," and one Lord's Day would be the focus of the second service every Sunday. In this way the basic teachings of the church were covered on an annual basis.
https://www.crcna.org/welcome/beliefs/confessions/heidelberg-catechism (accessed June 2, 2018).

15

The second of the three statements of faith of the Christian Reformed Church, the Belgic Confession of Faith was written in 1561 as a defense of the Protestant, Reformed faith against King Philip II of Spain, a Roman Catholic who sought to root out all Protestantism from those lands under his jurisdiction. https://www.crcna.org/welcome/beliefs/confessions/belgic-confession (accessed June 2, 2018).

16

The third doctrinal statement of the Christian Reformed Church is the Canons of Dort, adopted by the Synod (gathering of representatives from all the churches) held in the city of Dordrecht in the Netherlands, 1618-1619. The Canons of Dort contain the traditional "Five Points of Calvinism:" total depravity, unconditional election, limited atonement, irresistible grace, and perseverance of the saints. These five teachings are often referred to with the acronym TULIP. https://www.crcna.org/welcome/beliefs/confessions/canons-dort (accessed June 2, 2018).

17

In 1925 there were over 20,000 Klan members in Detroit. Herb Boyd, *Black Detroit: A People's History of Self-Determination* (New York: Harper Collins, 2017) 110.

18

Widick, *Detroit* 3.

19

David Maraniss, *Once in a Great City: A Detroit Story.* (New York: Simon & Schuster, 2015) 209.

20

See Chapter Five.

21

The 1943 riot was truly a race riot, with White people literally killing Black people because of the color of their skin. The 1967 riot, although larger and more destructive, was not simply a race riot. It was more an uprising of the poor of the city, many but not all of whom were Black, in rebellion against not sharing in the prosperity that other Americans were enjoying.

22

Stanley H. Brown, "Slow Healing of a City," Fortune, June 1965.

23

Lyndon Baines Johnson, *The Vantage Point: Perspectives of the Presidency 1963-1969*. (New York: Holt, Rinehart and Winston, 1971) 172.

24

William Scott III, *Hurt, Baby, Hurt* (Ann Arbor, MI: New Ghetto Press, Inc., 1970) 45. The book won the University of Michigan Hopwood Award in 1970.

25

Thomas A. Klug, "The Deindustrialization of Detroit" *Detroit 1967: Origins, Impacts, Legacies.* (Detroit: Wayne State University Press, 2017) 74.

26

Ibid., 66. Klug notes that this left the older, less efficient plants in the city where African-Americans worked. Klug writes: "Between 1947 and 1967, the number of production workers employed at manufacturing sites in Detroit shrank from 281,500 to 149,600 (47 percent). During the same period, production-worker employment outside the city in Wayne, Macomb, and Oakland Counties grew from 186,700 to 244,700, an increase of 58,000 (31 percent). The worst period of industrial job loss for Detroit occurred during the 1950s." Klug, p. 66. Michael R. Glass, *Cities in American Political History* Richardson Dalworth, ed. (Thousand Oaks, CA: CQ Press, 2011) notes "The relocation of jobs to these suburban areas occurred for at least two reasons. First, the land was inexpensive and could accommodate the large single-story buildings needed for modern production; second, spreading employment across a region could enhance a firm's ability to reduce union control, potentially preventing labor action on the scale witnessed in 1946 [which resulted in a 113 day strike]; and third, the new freeway system meant less reliance on the old transportation geographies, giving firms more freedom in choosing where they located their production facilities." p. 516. Today there are only 2 automobile factories in the city of Detroit: the GM Poletown plant and Chrysler's Jefferson North Assembly plant. Brad Plumber, "We saved the automakers. How come we didn't save Detroit? *The Washington Post,* July 19, 2013. https://www.washingtonpost.com/news/wonk/wp/2013/07/19/we-saved-

the-automakers-how-come-that-didnt-save-
detroit/?noredirect=on&utm_term=.21237fe8801d (accessed May 14,
2018).

27

Scott, Hurt, Baby, Hurt.

28

Allie Gross, "Detroit '67: 1966 Student Walkout at Northern a Sign of
Things to Come," *The Detroit Free Press*, July 16, 2017.
https://www.freep.com/story/news/local/michigan/detroit/2017/07/17/det
roit-67-1966-student-walkout-northern-sign-things-come/483019001/
(accessed June 3, 2018).

29

Henry David Thoreau, *On the Duty of Civil Disobedience* (London:
The Simple Life Press, 1903) 11.
https://books.google.com/books/about/On_the_Duty_of_Civil_Disobedie
nce.html?id=Nbq0bbBPUmoC&printsec=frontcover&source=kp_read_b
utton#v=onepage&q&f=false (accessed May 15, 2018).

30

Ibid, 19.

31

Robert D. McFaddon, *Samuel Brownell, 90, Ex-Education Official,
Dies.* New York Times, October 14, 1990.
https://www.nytimes.com/1990/10/14/obituaries/samuel-brownell-90-ex-
education-official-dies.html_ (last accessed November 16, 2018).

32

For more on the story of the Northern High School student walkout, see
Barry M. Franklin, "Community, Race and Curriculum in Detroit: The
Northern High School Walkout" chapter 3 in *Curriculum, Community,
and Urban School Reform* (New York: Macmillan, 2010) 57-79.

33

B.J. Widick, *Detroit: City of Race and Class Violence*, 156.

34

Herbert G. Locke, *The Detroit Riot of 1967.* (Detroit: Wayne State
University Press, 2017) 60.

35

John Stone, ed. *Detroit 1967: Origins, Impacts, Legacies*, 110.

36

Bill McGraw, *He helped start 1967 Detroit riot, now his son struggles with the legacy,* Bridge Magazine, https://www.freep.com/story/news/local/michigan/detroit/2016/12/29/detroit-riot-william-scott-race/95675688/ (accessed April 15, 2018), reprinted as Chapter 8 in *The Intersection: What Detroit Has Gained and Lost, 50 Years After the Uprisings of 1967,* Traverse City, MI: Mission Point Press, 2017.

37

Bill Scott tells his own story in a self-published memoir, *Hurt, Baby, Hurt* (Ann Arbor, MI: New Ghetto Press, Inc., 1970) which won the University of Michigan Hopwood Award in 1970.

38

"The Senseless Few," *The Detroit News,* July 24, 1967 p. 1.

39

Stone, *Detroit 1967,* 188.

40

Both cities, as well as the Michigan cities of Flint, Saginaw, Muskegon, Jackson, Ypsilanti, Mount Clemens, Pontiac, Lansing and Benton Harbor did experience similar disturbances that summer.

41

Stone, *Detroit 1967,* 161. Ken Coleman gives a good analysis of this issue in the chapter of this volume entitled, "Rebellion, Revolution, or Riot: The Debate Continues," 158-164. Note also B.J. Widick, who calls it a "social riot." He quotes Anthony Ripley, a spokesman for Mayor Cavanagh, who is quoted in the *Detroit Free Press,* July 26, 1967: "It is mostly a rebellion of people who have no stake in society, people in both races. You put up with the status quo as long as it works for you. If you are going nowhere and there is no end in sight, then hostility grows." Widick, *Detroit,* 168.

42

Rita Fields, "From Chaos to Clarity:How the Lessons Learned After the

Detroit Riot of 1967 Can Impact Effective Leadership Today," 26. https://www.academia.edu/10869797/From_Chaos_to_Clarity_How_the _Lessons_Learned_After_the_Detroit_Riot_of_1967_Can_Impact_Effec tive_Leadership_Today?email_work_card=interaction_paper (accessed April 18, 2020).

43

B.J. Widick, *Detroit, City of Race and Class Violence.* (Detroit: Wayne State University Press, 1989) 167, 171; Fields, "Chaos," 27.

44

Locke, *Riot,* 17.

45

"Mobs Burn and Loot 800 Stores; Troops Move In; Emergency Is On," The *Detroit Free Press,* July 24, 1967, p. 1.

46

Neal Rubin, "Dying for a smoke: The first fatality of the '67 riot." *The Detroit News* July 18, 2017. https://www.detroitnews.com/story/opinion/columnists/neal-rubin/2017/07/18/detroit-riot-first-fatality-grzanka/103815808. (accessed April 29, 2018). Note Widick, *Detroit*: "This was no race riot . . . Instead, it was a new sort of disorder: a social riot." 167.

47

Between the passage of the Armed Forces Reserve Act of 1952 and the Detroit riots of 1967, federal troops had been used five times domestically. Four of these instances dealt with desegregation of schools: September 23, 1957 Central High School, Little Rock AK; Sept. 30, 1962 the University of Mississippi; June 1963 the University of Alabama; 1963 Huntsville, Alabama. The fifth instance was the 1965 Selma to Montgomery Alabama Civil Rights march. In all five cases, the federal troops were sent to locations in South to enforce the civil rights of Negroes. In both the University of Alabama and the Selma Civil Rights march, Presidents Kennedy and Johnson federalized the Alabama National Guard. Jonathon Berlin and Kori Rumore, "12 Times the President Called in the Military Domestically," *The Chicago Tribune,* January 27, 2017 http://www.chicagotribune.com/news/ct-national-guard-deployments-timeline-htmlstory.html (accessed June 4, 2018).

48

Mayor Cavanaugh and the Black community leaders were also concerned about this issue before the State Police and National Guard were called in at 2 p.m. Sunday. Wick, *Detroit,* 170.

49

Lyndon Baines Johnson, *The Vantage Point: Perspectives on the Presidency 1963-1969.* New York: Holt, Rinehart and Winston, 1971) 168; Locke, *Riot,* 36.

50

Widick, *Detroit,* 170; "While Cities Burn," *New York Times,* July 26, 1967 p. 38.

51

Johnson, *Vantage Point,* 170.

52

Lyndon B. Johnson, *Remarks to the Nation After Authorizing the Use of Federal Troops in Detroit, July 24, 1967.*
http://www.presidency.ucsb.edu/ws/?pid=28364 (accessed June 4, 2018).

53

"Snipers vs. Machine Guns: Guerrilla War Rips 12th," The *Detroit News,* July 26, 1967 p. 1.

54

Locke, *Riot,* 39.

55

Lyndon B. Johnson, *July 24, 1967: Address After Ordering Federal Troops to Detroit, Michigan, https://millercenter.org/the-presidency/presidential-speeches/july-24-1967-address-after-ordering-federal-troops-detroit* (accessed November 23, 2019).

56

Oral interviews with Dave Cooke, April 2018 and Jack Nyenhuis, May 16, 2018.

57

Charlie LeDuff, *Detroit: An American Autoposy.* (New York: Penguin Press, 2013) p. 43.

58

Kevin Boyle, "The Rages of Whiteness: Racism, Segregation, and the Making of Modern Detroit," *Detroit 1967: Origins, Impacts, Legends* Joel Stone, ed. (Detroit: Wayne State University Press, 2017) 43.

59

James Evenhuis, *Detroit's Motor City Dutch,* https://dutchamericans.files.wordpress.com/2017/03/2003_02_evenhuis. pdf, p. 26 (accessed November 29, 2019).

60

Widick, *Detroit,* 25.

61

Ibid, 27.

62

Ibid, 27.

63

Ibid, 43.

64

James Evenhuis *Detroit's Motor City Dutch,* *https://dutchamericans.files.wordpress.com/2017/03/2003_02_evenhuis. pdf* (accessed June 3, 2020), 23.

65

First Christian Reformed Church of Detroit, "Historical Sketch" *Fiftieth Anniversary Booklet,* 1964, 3.

66

"Our History," *Historic Trinity Lutheran Church, Downtown Detroit.* https://www.historictrinity.org/our-history/   (accessed November 27, 2019).

67

*American Hungarian Reformed Church.* http://www.ahrchurch.org/history.html. (accessed November 27, 2019).

68

"History of Holy Trinity," *Holy Trinity Orthodox Church.*

https://holytrinitydetroit.org/history (accessed November 27, 2019).

69

Evenhuis Detroit's *Motor City Dutch,* 25.

70

Those who wanted Dutch services did not give up easily. In the summer of 1923, an appeal from the church was sent to the Classis (regional body of churches) on the issue of Dutch services.

71

Sugrue *The Origins of the Urban Crisis,* 44.

72

Rothstein, The *Color of Law,* 52.

73

Whether Eppinga and Hickly actually built the Sweet house is unknown. The house, built in 1919 and designed by Maurice Finkel is typical of many of the working class homes on Detroit's east side, including those built by Hickly and Eppinga. See Eric J. Hill, FAIA and John Gallagher, *AUA Detroit: The American Institute of Architects Guide to Detroit Architecture* (Detroit: Wayne State University Press, 2003) 282.

74

Ibid, 3.

75

Georgakas, Dan and Marvin Surkin. *Detroit: I Do Mind Dying* (Cambridge, MA: South End Press, 1998) 153, and Kenneth T. Jackson, *The Ku Klux Klan in the City, 1915-1930* (Chicago: Ivan R. Dee, 1992) 140.

76

Douglas O. Linder, *The Sweet Trials: An Account.* http://law2.umkc.edu/faculty/projects/ftrials/sweet/sweetaccount.HTM (accessed June 2, 2020).

77

Ibid

[78]

Ibid

[79] For the complete story of Ossian Sweet, see Phyllis Vine, *One Man's Castle: Clarence Darrow in Defense of the American Dream.* (New York; Harper Collins, 2004).

[80]

"National Housing Act (1934)." *The Living New Deal.* https://livingnewdeal.org/glossary/national-housing-act-1934/ (accessed December 9, 2019).

[81]

Boyle, "The Rages of Whiteness," 44.

[82]

Rothstein, *The Color of Law,* 65.

[83]

Ibid, 65.

[84]

Ibid, 65.

[85]

Sugrue, *The Origins of the Urban Crisis,* 47.

[86]

Ibid, 50.

[87]

Ibid, 50.

[88]

Ibid, 50.

[89]

Luke 4:18.

[90]

The Heidelberg Catechism, written in 1563 as a summary of Christian teaching from a Calvinist perspective. It's question and answer format was meant to educate both new converts and children. The students were expected to memorize the answers and recite them when the teacher asked the questions. The answer to question 74, "Should infants also be baptized?" is relevant here. According to the Catechism and therefore Christian Reformed doctrine, "by baptism, the sign of the covenant, they [children] too should be incorporated into the Christian church and distinguished from the children of unbelievers." https://www.crcna.org/welcome/beliefs/confessions/heidelberg-catechism (accessed June 11, 2020).

91

Lewis B. Smedes, *"My God and I: A Spiritual Memoir"* (Grand Rapids, MI: William B. Eerdman's, 2003) chapter 7.

92

See Exodus 16:3, KJV.

93

Written correspondence with Duane VanderBrug, June 9, 2020.

94

*Fiftieth Anniversary.*

95

Jeffrey Horner "Benefit of the Redoubt," *Detroit 1967: Origins, Impacts, Legends* Joel Stone, ed. (Detroit: Wayne State University Press, 2017) 83.

96

Telephone interview with Jarrett Bell, April 29, 2019.

97

*Fiftieth Anniversary.*

98

*Grosse Pointe Historical Society* http://www.gphistorical.org/mlk/mlkspeech/index.htm (accessed August 22, 2020).

99

Ibid

100

Luke 4:18-19.

101

I'm indebted to Richard Grevengoed for his written description of Harold Botts in an e-mail to me, May 19,2020.

102

*Fiftieth Anniversary.*

103

Cooke was admitted on his second try, a year later.

104

E-mail, April 20, 2020.

105

Telephone interview, December 4, 2019.

106

Interview, April 2019.

107

"African-Americans represented approximately 11 percent of the civilian population. Yet in 1967, they represented 16.3 percent of all draftees and 23 percent of all combat troops in Vietnam. In 1965, African-Americans accounted for nearly 25 percent of all combat deaths in Vietnam. By 1967 this percentage had dropped considerably, to 12.7, but the perception that Blacks were more likely to be drafted and killed remained widespread." Gerald F. Goodwin, "Black and White in Vietnam." *New York Times,* July 18, 2017. https://www.nytimes.com/2017/07/18/opinion/racism-vietnam-war.html (accessed August 3, 2020).

108

I am indebted to Bill VanderVliet (one of the SWIMers), David Cooke, Sr., Dave Cooke Jr., Mel VanderBrug, Rich Grevengoed, Jarrett Bell, and Suki Botts (daughter of Harold Botts) for telling me the stories of the experiences of the Community Church during the rebellion in oral interviews.

109

Time Magazine, April 25, 1960, p.25.

110

Cosseboom, Grosse *Pointe, Michigan: Race Against Race* (Lansing, MI: Michigan State University Press, 1972)  5.

111

Ibid, 6.

112

"Michigan Fights Real Estate Ban." *New York Times,* June 5, 1960, p. R1.  "Grosse Pointe's Gross Points" *Time Magazine*, April 25, 1960 p. 25.

113

Ibid, 7.

114

"Michigan Fights Real Estate Ban." *New York Times,* June 5, 1960, p. R1.

115

"Michigan Orders Point System End: Screening of Prospective Home Buyers Denounced by Attorney General." *New York Times,* May 15, 1960, p. 81.

116

Cosseboom, *Grosse Pointe, Michigan: Race Against Race* (Lansing, MI: Michigan State University Press, 1972) 16.

117

Ibid, 24.

118

*Grosse Pointe Civil Rights Organizations: Papers, 1963-1973.* (Detroit: Archives of Labor and Urban Affairs, Accession Number 1456). https://reuther.wayne.edu/files/UR001456.pdf.  Last accessed April 19, 2019.

119

"Whites and Negroes Join In Demonstration Against Housing

Discrimination." *Grosse Pointe News,* July 4, 1963.
http://digitize.gp.lib.mi.us/digitize/newspapers/gpnews/1960-
64/63/1963-07-04.pdf. (accessed April 20, 2019).

120

Ibid

121

Cosseboom, *Grosse Pointe, Michigan,* 7.

122

Ibid

123

State of Michigan Civil Rights Commission letter to the Residents of
Grosse Pointe Woods, July 22, 1966. Records Relating to Housing, file
74-90, Michigan State Archives, Lansing, MI.

124

*Opening Doors: Grosse Pointe Committee for Open Housing Newsletter,*
Grosse Pointe Civil Rights Organizations: Papers, 1963-1973. Assession
Number 1456. Walter P. Reuther Library, Archives of Labor and Urban
Affairs, Wayne State University.

125

"G. Pointers Meet and Quietly Accept their First Negro," The *Detroit
News,* July 27, 1966, p. 1A.

126

"First Grosse Pointe Negroes Find Insults are Abating." *The Detroit
Free Press,* Wednesday, July 27, 1966, p. 3.

127

Cosseboom, *Grosse Pointe, Michigan,* 56.

128

Ibid, 60.

129

Quoted in Herb Boyd, *Black Detroit: A People's History of Self-
Determination* (New York: Harper Collins, 2017) 95.

130

Abraham Kuyper, *The Problem of Poverty.* Edited and translated by James W. Skillen. (Grand Rapids, MI: Baker, 1991) 51.

131

Dilworth, Richard. *Cities in American Political History.*

132

Gary K. Clabaugh, "Thunder on the Right: The Protestant Fundamentalists" https://www.carlmcintire.org/other-thunder.php (last accessed November 27, 2018).

133

"History," Christian Reformed Church website, https://www.crcna.org/welcome/history#toc_(accessed December 1, 2018).

134

"First Christian Reformed Church of Detroit: 50th Anniversary 1914-1964."

135

John F. Kennedy, "Address to Joint Session of Congress, May 25, 1961" https://www.jfklibrary.org/learn/about-jfk/historic-speeches/address-to-joint-session-of-congress-may-25-1961 (last accessed November 27, 2018).

136

James H. Cone, "The White Church and Black Power" in *Black Theology: A Documentary History, 1966-1979,* ed. Gayraund S. Whilmore and James H. Cone. (Maryknoll, New York: Orbis Books, 1979) 117.

137

Naraj Warikoo, "Black Madonna Turned Church into Social Force." *The Detroit Free Press,* April 8, 2017. https://www.freep.com/story/news/local/michigan/detroit/2017/04/27/detroit-shrine-Black-madonna/100947864/ (accessed January 14, 2020).

138

In 1978 the church was again renamed the Shrine of the Black Madonna of the Pan-African Orthodox Christian Church.

139

"First Christian Reformed Church of Detroit: 50th Anniversary 1914-1964."

140

From an oral interview with Jim Groenewold, June 16, 2018 in Waupon, Wisconsin.

141

Mary Helen Schaafsma, *First Christian Reformed Church of Detroit 100th Anniversary Book,* Heritage Hall (Heckman Library) Calvin University, Grand Rapids MI.

[142] A copy of the program for that service can be found in the Calvin College Archive, Grand Rapids MI.

143

Oral interview with Stacy Steen, December 6, 2018.

144

Ibid

145

Reverend Duane VanderBrug in a note to the author, July 14, 2020.

146

Ibid

147

Millard Lampell and George Kleinsinger, *Pass it On.* Copyright Universal Music Publishing, Chicago.

148

Quoted in Chartier, Myron Raymond, "The Social Views of Dwight L. Moody and Their Relation to the Workingman of 1860-1900" (1969). Fort Hays Studies Series. 40. https://scholars.fhsu.edu/fort_hays_studies_series/40 (accessed June 23, 2020).

149

Abraham Kuyper, *Problem of Poverty,* trans. James W. Skillen. (Sioux Center, IA: Dordt College Press, 2011) 61.

150

Abraham Kuyper, *Calvinism: Six Stone-lectures.* New York: Fleming H. Revell Company, 1898) 31.

151

Michael R. Wagenman, *Engaging the World with Abraham Kuyper.* (Bellingham, WA: Lexham Press, 83).

152

Lisa Marder, *A Deep Dive Into the History of the Social Gospel Movement: Religious Teachings Meet Social Justice Reform.* https://www.learnreligions.com/social-gospel-movement-4136473 (accessed June 23, 2020).

153

I'm indebted for this observation to Stacey Steen in an Oral Interview, December 6, 2018.

154

Minutes of the Grosse Pointe Christian School Board, June 28, 1967.

155

Cosseboom, Grosse *Pointe, Michigan,* 95.

156

For a more complete account of the Lawndale/Timothy Christian School incident, see Christopher H. Meehan, *Growing Pains: How Racial Struggles Changed a Church and a School.* (Grand Rapids: William B. Eerdmans Publishing Company, 2017).

157

Interview with Shirley Verspoor, May 21, 2019, Grand Rapids MI and Board member Curtis Vrieland Gun Lake MI April 28, 2019. Curtis Vrieland is the father of the author of this book.

158

The story of Shirley Verspoor comes from both the author's memory and an oral interview with her in her home, Grand Rapids, MI. May 21, 2019.

159

Minutes of the Grosse Pointe Christian School Board, August 30, 1967.

160

Ibid

161

Heidelberg Catechism, Question and Answer 74. https://www.crcna.org/welcome/beliefs/confessions/heidelberg-catechism (accessed May 2, 2019)

162

Ibid

163

Minutes of the Grosse Pointe Christian School Board, September 27, 1967.

164

Ibid

165

Minutes of the Grosse Pointe Christian School Board, November 29, 1967.

166

Minutes, January 31, 1968.

167

"Hubbard, Orville." *The Detroit Historical Society Encyclopedia of Detroit. https://detroithistorical.org/learn/encyclopedia-of-detroit/hubbard-orville* (accessed May 1, 2019).

168

The questions of race were obviously troubling to both the Dearborn Church and School. On May 7, 1968 the Dearborn Church sent the following official request (Overture) to the regional body of churches, Classis Lake Erie: "The Dearborn consistory overtures Classis to appoint a committee to draw up a suggested list of reference materials (books, articles, pamphlets, tapes, films, etc.) for use by churches and individuals of Classis to assist them in studying and facing the racial problem with Christian objectivity and involvement." The Classis approved the overture and appointed a three-man committee, including Reverend Botts, to assemble the materials. The Dearborn Christian School eventually did accept Black Students from the Community Church.

169

Minutes, April 24, 2019.

170

Minutes, May 29, 1968.

171

Ibid

172

Ibid

173

Ibid

174

Minutes, 39th Annual School Society Meeting June 17, 1968.

175

Minutes, August 21, 1968.

176

Minutes, June 26, 1968.

177

Minutes, August 21, 1968.

178

I could find no verification of this in the records, but I remember the incident and others who were part of the Community Church confirmed my memory.

179

Ibid

180

Jude Huetteman, "The Night MLK Came to Grosse Pointe."
*The Detroit Free Press,* January 14, 2018.
https://www.freep.com/story/opinion/contributors/2018/01/14/martin-luther-king-grosse-pointe/1030581001/ (accessed January 25, 2020).

181

"Letters to the Editor," *Grosse Pointe News,* March 28, 1968, page 24.

182

*American Rhetoric: Top 100 Speeches.*
https://www.americanrhetoric.com/speeches/mlkihaveadream.htm
(accessed August 22, 2020).

183

Jenn M. Jackson, "Martin Luther King Was More Radical Than We Remember," *Teen Vogue,* January 15, 2018.
https://www.teenvogue.com/story/mlk-more-radical-than-we-remember?utm_medium=social&mbid=social_facebook&utm_social-type=owned&utm_source=facebook&utm_brand=tv&fbclid=IwAR22X-JFeSx3pUH4ZJR03YOK7YB3IV37XW80YOgh2IiIDSAF0CrJ7uu85lw (accessed January 21, 2020).

184

Ed Clayton, Martin *Luther King: The Peaceful Warrior* (Englewood Cliffs, NJ: Prentice-Hall Inc., 1964).

185

Huetteman, "The Night MLK Came to Grosse Pointe."

186

A copy of the mailing can be found in the Grosse Pointe Civil Rights Organizations Records, Assession 1456, Box #1, Folder #6, Walter P. Reuther Library, Archives of Labor and Urban Affairs, Wayne State University.

187

Dan Georgakas and Marvin Surkin, *Detroit, I Do Mind Dying,* 3rd. Ed. (Chicago, Haymarket Books, 2012) p. 53 observe, "Breakthrough's Donald Lobsinger . . . went around organizing openly racist and anti-Semitic groups reminiscent of the Black Legion that had terrorized Detroiters in the 1930s."

188

Donald Lobsinger, oral interview with William Winkel, St Clair Shores, MI June 23rd, 2016. https://detroit1967.detroithistorical.org/items/show/287 (accessed July 1, 2020).

189

A copy of the flier can be found in the Grosse Pointe Civil Rights Organizations Records, Assession 1456, Box #1, Folder #6, Walter P. Reuther Library, Archives of Labor and Urban Affairs, Wayne State University.

190

"George Wallace's Detroit Visit Provokes Police Brutality." *The History Engine.* https://historyengine.richmond.edu/episodes/view/6625 (accessed February 20, 2020).

191

"School Board Meeting Heated: King Lecture, Election Set Up Argument." *Grosse Pointe News,* March 14, 1968, p. 1.

192

The entire speech can be found at http://www.aavw.org/special_features/speeches_speech_king01.html (accessed January 30, 2020).

193

David Levering Lewis, *King: A Biography,* 3rd. ed. (Chicago: University of Illinois Press, 2013) 373.

194

The entire sermon is available at https://kinginstitute.stanford.edu/king-papers/documents/drum-major-instinct-sermon-delivered-ebenezer-baptist-church (accessed January 31, 2020).

195

Lewis, *King: A Biography* p, 377.

196

Tavis Smiley, *Death of a King: The Real Story of Dr. Martin Luther King*

*Jr's Final Year* (New York: Little, Brown and Company, 2014) 191.

197

For the complete text of the speech, see Grosse Pointe Historical Society, The *Other America.* https://www.gphistorical.org/mlk/mlkspeech/ (accessed February 4, 2020). To compare with the Stanford University speech, see Aurora Forum at Stanford University 15 April 2007. https://auroraforum.stanford.edu/files/transcripts/Aurora_Forum_Transcript_Martin_Luther_King_The_Other_America_Speech_at_Stanford_04.15.07.pdf (accessed February 2, 2020)

198

Huetteman, "The Night MLK Came to Grosse Pointe."

199

Lewis, *King: A Biography* p. 376.

200

Ibid, 380.

201

Raphael Warnock, "Dreams from our Fathers," in *The Audacity of Faith: Christian Leaders Reflect on the Election of Barack Obama,* ed. M.A. McMickle (Valey Forge, PA: Judson Press, 2009), 65.

202

J.D. Vance, *Hillbilly Elegy: A Memoir of a Family and Culture in Crisis,* 255.

203

Drew Philip, *A $500 House in Detroit: Rebuilding an Abandoned Home and an American City.* (New York: Scribner,2017), 5.

204

United States Census Bureau estimate, July 1, 2019. https://www.census.gov/quickfacts/grossepointeparkcitymichigan (accessed July 31, 2020).

205

Beginning in the 1940s, the night before Halloween has been known as

"Devil's Night" in the city.  It was a night where youth would roam the streets and engage in harmless forms of vandalism: throwing eggs at houses and toilet paper in the trees.  Beginning in the 1970s, the vandalism increased and included arson in inner-city neighborhoods. In the early 1980s, as many as 800 fires were reported in the city on Devil's Night.

206

Katherine Gowman observes,  "Since the 1980s, physical barriers have been erected by Grosse Pointe's city planning department to further isolate the suburb and protect it from Detroit.  Of the twelve streets that cross Altar Road, connecting Detroit to Grosse Pointe, four have been physically blocked off, three are without direct access into Detroit, two are one-way streets, two run adjacent to the front and rear of the main police station, and the last remaining street is approved to be closed.  A continuing physical and psychological segregation at the Alter Road border has been quietly but efficiently implemented."  Katherine Gowman, *The Other America.* https://the-other-america.com/barricades/pjmo2as0w0tecxhuixk6j44dtqg2z8 (accessed July 1, 2020).

207

Telephone interview with Jarrett Bell, April 9, 2019.